Weapons of Delta Force

Fred J. Pushies

ZENITH
PRESS

Dedication

To the Operators

First published in 2002 by Zenith Press, an imprint of MBI Publishing Company, 400 First Avenue North, Suite 300, Minneapolis, MN 55401 USA

Zenith Press titles are also available at discounts in bulk quantity for industrial or sales-promotional use. For details write to Special Sales Manager at MBI Publishing Company, 400 First Avenue North, Suite 300, Minneapolis, MN 55401 USA.

To find out more about our books, visit us online at www.zenithpress.com.

ISBN-13: 978-0-7603-3824-7

The Library of Congress has cataloged the hardcover edition as follows:

Pushies, Fred J., 1952-
Weapons of Delta Force / Fred J. Pushies
            p. cm.
Includes index.
ISBN 0760311390 (PLC)
1. United States. Army. Delta Force. 2. Unites States Army—Weapons system. 3. Military weapons—United States. I. Title.
UA34.S64 P8723 2002
623.4/0973--dc21
                            2002072089

On the front cover: Clockwise from upper left: Soldier with an M136 AT4 anti-tank weapon, an HK USP .45 caliber ACP, soldier with a Colt M4A1 carbine with Trijicon Relfex Sight, and an HK416. The HK416 is a new tool in the global war on terrorism, developed primarily as an improvement to the M4A1. The HK416 uses a piston rod operating system instead of the direct impingement system of the M16/M4 family of weapons. This improves accuracy and is cleaner, resulting in less operator maintenance. The HK416 is battle proven with Delta in Southwest Asia. This HK416 is equipped with a 10.39 inch barrel, AN/PEQ-2 Target Pointer/Illuminator/Aiming Light (TPIAL), EOTech holographic weapon sight, vertical fore-grip, and SOPMOD stock. *Heckler & Koch*

On the frontispiece: As in the beginning, over two decades ago, Delta Force still draws many of its operators from the ranks of the U.S. Army Special Forces—the "Green Berets." Experts in Direct Action (DA), Special Reconnaissance (SR), Counterterrorism (CT), and Foreign Internal Defense (FID), they are the perfect pool from which to draw. These highly skilled and motivated individuals bring a valuable asset to the Delta organization.

On the title page: This CT stack prepares to blow the door and perform a dynamic entry into the building. The team has placed explosive cutting tape on the door, which, when detonated, will provide them with an unhindered opening; it also will serve to distract and disorient any hostile on the other side of the door.

On the back cover: (Main) Rubber Duck operations from an MH-47E. (Inset) Delta operators are skilled in an assortment of infil methods, whether from sea, air, or land.

Editor: Sara Perfetti
Design Manager: Brenda C. Canales
Designed by: Stephanie Michaud
Cover designed by: Matthew Simmons

Printed in China

Contents

Acknowledgments

I would like to thank God for the privilege of living in a country that is free. May He bless this great nation of the United States of America! May He grant peace to our homeland, wisdom to our leaders, and protection to those who mete out the infinite justice of that wisdom upon our enemies. Many people with a solid working relationship with the Special Operations Community in general, and Delta specifically, assisted in this work. As real world events unfolded on 11 September 2001, I was concerned about mentioning them by name. In consideration of operational and personal security, I contacted several sources regarding this topic. The consensus approved company involvement but asked for no mention of specific persons.

I would like to thank those who gave of their time and experience and provided contacts, data, photos, and even equipment to reveal an inside look at the tools of this ultra-elite unit. I offer personal thanks to those close to the project, who shall remain nameless, else my head may end up in someone's refrigerator. I would also like to express my thanks to the following companies for their help in this project: MOSA Sports; New Eagle International; Blackhawk Industries, Inc.; Wilson Combat; Bolle; Knight Armament Company; Trijicon; Aimpoint; EOTech; Lance Ordnance; Benelli; GEMTECH; Mossberg; Eagle; Specialty Defense; Rings Manufacturing; Special Technology Systems; Motorola; Sonetronics, Inc.; Thales Communications; ICOM America, Inc.; Insight Technology; TEA; Heckler & Koch; Universal Propulsion Com-pany; Litton; Rockwell-Collins; ITT; Raytheon; Night Vision Equipment Company; Wilcox; Military Manufac-turing Company; Remington; Colt; Combined Tactical Systems; Telex Communications; Sikorsky Helicopters; Boeing; MD Helicopters.

Finally, I would like to thank the many people who provided me with direction, tidbits of data, or contacts during the course of my producing this work. There are also numerous individuals and companies who helped but requested to remain in the shadows, much like the operators they supply. To them, I also express my gratitude; for talking to me off the record, they shall remain in anonymity. To my editor, Sara Perfetti, and MBI Publishing, my thanks. I want to thank the CGG for its support, and my family and friends who provided encouragement.

Introduction

When you mention the term counterterrorism (CT), images come to mind of assault teams clothed in black outfits and balaclavas, wielding exotic-looking weaponry. Around the globe, governments have established organizations of men and women committed to neutralizing continually growing terrorist activities. For instance, units with extraordinary chutzpah like the Israelis' crack anti-terrorist elements, the British Special Air Service (SAS), Germany's GSG9, and others are actively engaged in CT missions. Of all these CT units, there remains one that is shrouded in secrecy and commands awe. A unit so secret, its members are required to sign nondisclosure agreements promising not to discuss its existence. A unit so exact in meting out America's National Command Authority (NCA) missions that the mere mention they are being deployed has brought more than one crisis to a hasty conclusion. This organization of hand-selected, highly motivated, specially trained, superbly equipped, and experienced professionals forms the unit officially known as the 1st Special Forces Operational Detachment–DELTA, more commonly referred to as **Delta Force.**

Contact the Public Affairs Office at the U.S. Army Special Operations Command at Fort Bragg in North Carolina and ask about Delta, and if whomever answers doesn't hang up on you, he will say, "Delta is an airline." Search the Internet, and you'll find several sites dedicated to the "Force," yet veiled in obscurity. The U.S. Department of Defense simply comments, ". . . It is classified." End of discussion.

When you refer to the Israelis you think of Operation Jonathan, the raid on Entebbe, Uganda, in 1976. Mention the British SAS and images of Princess Gate in England come to mind. Delta's premier moment in the spotlight came on 24 May 1980, in the Iranian wasteland, a location known as Desert One. This was the assembly point for Operation Eagle Claw, the mission to rescue American hostages at the U.S. embassy in Teheran, Iran. While many critics and armchair commandos considered this a total failure, it was not without powerful lessons learned and many profound acts of courage by all participants. Considering the mission and the resources available at that time in history, the fact that the assault team was assembled at Desert One was an accomplishment in itself.

I would not want to be in the Iranians' kaffiyehs, should this mission be carried out today. Considering Delta's deadly capabilities, coupled with the lethality of U.S. Special Operations Command (USSOCOM) assets at its disposal, the mission would certainly have a different outcome. Any terrorists or enemies of the United States with an ounce of gray matter should be sure their affairs are in order before they commit an act of aggression. Indeed, the hostiles may get our attention, but if Delta is deployed we will certainly get the last word.

As you, the reader, go through the pages of this book you will see a sampling of the weapons and equipment used by Delta Force operators. The focus of this work is on the weapons, not the internal workings and operations of the Force. In consideration of OPSEC (operational security), the presentation or description of a weapon system or technique may use an image of an alternative U.S. SOF shooter. Am I presenting every weapon in the armory? No. Is there a weapon or piece of equipment we have missed? Probably; nevertheless, this information was gathered from those who shall remain nameless, and who are considered informed and reliable sources. If you are in possession of a drawerful of Delta photos, or are a Delta operator past or present, feel free to contact me through my publisher, and we'll consider doing a Volume II. For it is the musician who creates the music, not the instrument; the surgeon who operates, not the scalpel; hence, while the Rangers may also use the M4A1 in the science of warfare, it is raised to a new level of lethality when in the hands of the Delta operator. It is not the intention of this work or author to compromise any operators, but merely to present the tools of their trade and to honor this unit for its outstanding missions and accomplishments. While some operations have come to light in the past few years, most will remain forever hidden in the classified files and in the experiences of the warrior's soul.

History and Background

The best of the best! As in the beginning, over two decades ago, Delta Force still draws many of its operators from the ranks of the U.S. Army Special Forces— "The Green Berets." Experts in Direct Action (DA), Special Reconnaissance (SR), Counterterrorism (CT), and Foreign Internal Defense (FID), they are the perfect pool from which to draw. These highly skilled and motivated individuals bring a valuable asset to the Delta organization.

Operation Eagle Claw

In November 1979 a group of Iranian "students" captured the U.S. embassy in Teheran, Iran. The Air Force rushed to regenerate its special operations capabilities. By December 1979 a rescue force was chosen and training commenced. Training exercises were conducted through March 1980 and on 16 April 1980, the Joint Chiefs of Staff (JCS) approved the mission. On 19 April, the rescue forces, consisting of Army, Navy, Air Force, and Marine assets, began to deploy to Southwest Asia. Delta Force would be tasked with the assault on the embassy and the rescue of the American hostages.

On 24 April, after six months of failed negotiations, the National Command Authorities (NCA) ordered the execution of Operation Eagle Claw to free U.S. hostages held in Iran. Under the cover of darkness, eight RH-53D helicopters departed the USS *Nimitz* on station in the Arabian Sea; at the same time six C-130s left Masirah Island, Oman. Both sets of aircraft set off for a prearranged site 600 miles into the desert wasteland, code designation Desert One. The Achilles' heels in the operation were the helicopters. A few hours into the mission, two helicopters had aborted due to mechanical failure. A desert dust storm, known as a "Haboob" caused the

Two RH-53D helicopters are brought up to the deck in preparation for Operation Eagle Claw. While appearing as a military debacle, the operation would prove to be a watershed for U.S. Special Operation Forces, and Delta in particular. *Defense Visual Information Center*

remaining helicopters to arrive late; and yet another suffered a hydraulic leak that its crew determined to be unfixable at the Desert One site. This determination resulted in only five operational helicopters. Mission planners had ascertained a minimum of six helicopters were required for the mission to continue, now with only five available, the mission had to be aborted.

With the decision to abort, it was time to load up the aircraft and "get out of Dodge." While repositioning his RH-53D helicopter for refueling, one of the pilots collided with a C-130. This resulted in the two aircraft rapidly being engulfed in flames. With the situation hastily moving from bad to worse to disastrous, the on-scene commander, Col. Charlie Beckwith, decided to load all the survivors—remaining troops, assault team, and Marine air crews on the C-130—and depart Desert One ASAP! Eight men had been killed and five more injured. They left behind five intact helicopters, the burned wreckage of the helicopter and C-130, and the dead. Operation Eagle Claw had failed. This had cost the lives of eight gallant troops; it would cost the honor of the United States of America, and it would cost the credibility of U.S. Special Operations.

Many books and articles have been written describing the mission in detail, so we will not belabor the operation here. Very simply stated: The plan was to assemble eight Navy RH-53D helicopters at Desert One. Under the cover of darkness, the helicopters would be refueled from KC-130 tankers, which would also land in the desert, load a 120-man Army assault team and proceed to two additional hide sites. The Delta assault team would proceed to the U.S. embassy, extract the hostages, rendezvous with the helicopters, and be extracted from the city. In actuality, the Delta operators never got to carry out *their* mission, the rescue of the hostages.

Following the disaster at Desert One, a review committee, known as the Holloway Commission, chaired by Adm. James L. Holloway III, including Gen. LeRoy Manor, who commanded the Son Tay raid into North Vietnam, convened to look into problems within U.S. Special Operations. The outcome of this commission resulted in two major recommendations.

RH-53D helicopters prepare for departure from the USS *Nimitz*, their destination a clandestine location in the Iranian desert, code designation Desert One. On 24 April, Operation Eagle Claw, the mission to free U.S. hostages held in Iran, had commenced. The mission, which began as a courageous attempt, ended in disaster. *Defense Visual Information Center*

First, the Department of Defense (DOD) should establish a Counter Terrorism Joint Task Force (CTJTF) as a field organization of the Joint Chiefs of Staff with a permanently assigned staff and forces. The JCS would plan, train for, and conduct operations to counter terrorist activities directed against the United States. The CTJTF would utilize military forces in the counter terrorism (CT) role.

These forces could range in size from small units of highly specialized personnel to larger integrated forces. Second, the JCS should consider the formation of a Special Operations Advisory Panel (SOAP). This panel would consist of high-ranking officers to be drawn from both active service and retired personnel. The prerequisite for selection was a background in special operations or having served at a Commander in Chief (C in C) or JCS level and having maintained a proficient level of interest in special operations or defense policy.

One issue raised by the commission concerned the selection of helicopter air crews. Were the pilots up to the task? Why had they selected the Marines when more than 100 qualified Air Force H-53 pilots were available? If we look at today's standards, the Marine pilots had big boots to fill. They were being asked to fly at night; this alone was unusual practice for the "flying leathernecks." These pilots were now being asked to perform the extraordinary. Launch off the deck of a carrier, *at night*; fly (NOE) where radar could not detect them and with no running lights. The pilots were issued PVS5 night-vision goggles; however, they could only be worn at 30-minute intervals. This meant the pilot and co-pilot had to alternate flying the huge helicopter every 30 minutes. The Marines had no pilots that had been trained in this type of flying. In fact, none of the services were prepared for such a contingency.

Regarding the helicopters: The commission concluded that a minimum of 10 to 12 helicopters should have been deployed. This redundancy in air assets would have secured a higher probability of success should problems have arisen, resulting in a minimum of six operational helicopters at Desert One, which was the minimum requirement for the completion of the mission. This legacy may prove to hamper future special operations. It is this commission's direction that spawned interest in the V-22 Osprey, redesignated the MV-22 and CV-22 for use among Marine and Special Operations Forces (SOF). Many Osprey evangelists believe that the Osprey will aspire to a principal SOF air asset and infiltration/exfiltration (Infil/Exfil) platform. The only problem is, the dang thing won't seem to stay in the air and has already cost the lives of more than 20 troops. Oh—and you can not seem to fit any type of ground-support vehicle in the Special Ops (or entire U.S. Military) inventory inside: no Fast Attack Vehicles (FAV), no HUMMVs, not even the AFSOC, or Rapid All Terrain Transport (RATT), can be deployed inside the aircraft. However, you can fit six of them on the deck of an aircraft carrier. Time will tell whether the Osprey will have a place in the Special Ops inventory, or end up hanging in the U.S. Air Force Museum in Dayton, Ohio.

Another issue was the lack of a thorough readiness assessment and schedule of mission rehearsals. From the onset, training was not conducted in a truly joint method. Due to security and logistical considerations, the training was compartmentalized and held at scattered locations across the continental United States, as well as abroad. The limited rehearsals conducted could only evaluate various segments of the entire mission. Additionally, preparation was carried out at the individual and unit level within each element.

There was no designated mission commander for six months, breaching the principle of unity of command. This lack of command and control hampered the training, planning, and execution of the operation. There were separate commanders for site security, ground force, landing support, KC-130s, and the helicopter force. Compounding the problem were procedural limitations and lack of communications interoperability.

While the mission itself ended in disaster, you can truly not cast blame on Delta. In reality, members of the force did not get up to bat, so while they did not hit a home run, neither did they strike out. Indeed, Desert One would serve as a catalyst for the evolution of the U.S. Special Operations Forces, and a foundation upon which Delta Force would rise up to become the formidable force it is today.

USSOCOM

Over two decades have passed since the Desert One initiative. Today, America Special Operation Forces are par excellence and second to none. There is no greater light infantry unit in the world than the U.S. Army Rangers. The U.S. Army Special Forces—"The Green Berets"— are deployed in numerous countries of the free world, and some not so free. The activities of the U.S. Navy SEALs are legendary. The air assets of the 160th Special Operations Aviation Regiment (Airborne) (SOAR(A)) and Air Force Special Operations Command (AFSOC) are equipped with the latest technology, and the pilots/air crews are the best in the world.

Overseeing all of the U.S. Special Operations Forces is the U.S. Special Operations Command (USSOCOM), located at McDill Air Force Base in Tampa, Florida. Each of the three services, Army, Air

Delta Force routinely holds open recruitment twice a year. While any Army MOS (Military Occupational Specialty) may apply for selection into Delta, a high percentage of those selected come from the Ranger battalions. The U.S. Army Rangers are a natural progression in the Special Operations Forces. It is not unusual to see the Ranger tab just under the Special Forces Qualification tab worn by many of the Delta operators.

Force, and Navy, has a subordinate command to SOCOM. An additional subordinate command under SOCOM is the Joint Special Operations Command, (JSOC). According to the United States Special Operations Forces Posture Statement, JSOC "is a joint headquarters designed to study special operations requirements and techniques, ensure interoperability and equipment standardization, plan and conduct special operations exercises and training; and develop joint special operations tactics." Activated in 1981 at Fort Bragg, North Carolina, JSOC's mission was to consolidate control of, and help develop special operations doctrine for, training, deployment, and other CT missions. Since that time its mission has expanded to encompass direct action (DA) missions, which require unique skills of its operators. It has also relocated to Pope Air Force Base,

next door to Fort Bragg, just south of Green Ramp.

Delta Force is officially designated as the 1st Special Forces Operational Detachment—DELTA. The unit also has a cover name and is known as the Combat Applications Group, or CAG. The official comments from SOCOM on CAG states, "Effective 1 October 1991, the U.S. Army Combat Applications Group (Airborne) was activated as a subordinate element of the U.S. Army Special Operations Command (USASOC). Formed during the restructuring of Army special operations assets, the CAG (Abn) tests special operations methods, equipment, tactics, and combined arms interoperability with a focus of the development of doctrine beyond the year 2000."

Delta Force has also evolved over the years into a force to be reckoned with. Delta was organized in the late 1970s under the command of Col. "Chargin' Charlie" Beckwith. The unit was headquartered in the Fort Bragg Stockade building. It even could trace its lineage to the Office of Strategic Service (OSS) of World War II, as some of the evaluation tests given to OSS agents are also required during the selection process of Delta candidates. The many lessons Col. Beckwith learned during his exchange with the British SAS set the standards for the troops then as well as for future operators.

Today's Delta has moved from the stockade and has relocated to a more

Land navigation is indispensable to a Delta operator. During the selection process, candidates will undergo numerous exercises to instill and hone this proficiency. Delta operators are experts at using a map and a compass, as well as celestial navigation, that is using the stars. Although they are issued GPS units and are quite adept in their use, they must always be able to travel from point to point relying on traditional alternatives.

While Delta maintains a high level of secrecy, it does offer open recruitment from time to time. Delta will travel to various military installations to seek individuals who may have what it takes and possess the needed skills to become a member of the unit. Part of the orientation at the Special Forces Non Commissioned Officers Academy includes a presentation from the Delta recruiter.

Although the Department of Defense categorically states that any reference to Delta Force is completely classified, it makes no secret as to the recruitment of its members. Delta conducts worldwide recruitment campaigns twice each year just prior to its spring and fall Asses-sment-and-Selection Course. Due to the very nature of the Force, and the missions performed, Delta operators are carefully screened, evaluated, selected, and trained. The assessment process evaluates whether the candidate possesses the necessary stamina, dedication, and self-discipline to perform the unique and arduous tasks required of Delta members—while simultaneously enduring physical and psychological stress. Both officers and NCOs undergo the identical assessment, selection, and training.

The general prerequisites for officers and NCOs are the following: volunteer; Army active duty, Reserve, or National Guard; male; U.S. citizen; passing a HALO/SCUBA physical and eye examination; no limiting physical profile; airborne-qualified or volunteer for airborne training; passing a background security investigation and having a minimum clearance of SECRET; minimum age of 22; no history of recurring disciplinary action; passing the five-event physical-fitness qualification test (inverted crawl; run, dodge, and jump; pushups; situps; two-mile run; and 100-meter swim—all while wearing BDU and boots).

NCO prerequisites: rank of sergeant (E-5) through sergeant first class (E-7), four years minimum time in service, passing SQT score in primary Military Occupational Specialty (MOS), minimum GT score of 110, two years active service remaining upon selection.

Officer prerequisites: captain or major (branch immaterial); advanced-course graduate; college graduate (B.A. or B.S.); minimum of 12 months successful command (company, battery, troop, Special Force A-detachment, or aviation platoon).

Assessment and Selection is completed in three to four weeks and is divided into three phases. During this time the candidate will endure numerous physical-fitness exercises, including an 18-mile "ruck march" carrying 40 to 45 pounds in his rucksack. This is a timed march and must be completed within four and a half hours or less. The next phase is advanced land navigation. This brings all the individuals up to speed and prepares them for the third phase. Even in this modern age of GPS, the candidate must be proficient with a map and compass; it is mandatory for each candidate to master these skills. Finally, Phase III, which mirrors many of the tasks the British SAS carry out, as its recruits shoulder a Bergen and traverse the Brecon Beacons in Wales. In this test of endurance and mental stamina, the individuals carry a 40–45 pound rucksack and navigate their assigned routes. Each day the distance varies, from 7 to 40 miles. All of the objectives must be met in order for the candidate to pass and continue in the selection process.

Upon successful completion of these three phases, the individual undergoes a thorough psychological testing and evaluation conducted by Delta psychologists. Finally, the soldier will have an interview with the Commanders Board. Candidates selected will usually register PCS (Permanent Change of Station) to Ft. Bragg within a month or two.

Having passed the Assessment and Selection Course and been accepted into the Force, officers and NCOs will now enter into the Operators Training Course (OTC), which last six months. It is here that the new Delta members are schooled in the skills required for placement in a Delta Team as an "operator." Training ranges from basic to advanced levels of weapons training and marksmanship: shoot/no-shoot skills known as selective firing; combat skills; CQB; defensive and evasive driving techniques; demolitions; breaching obstacles; first aid; Infil/Exfil techniques; climbing and abseiling parachuting (static and HALO), survival, escape, resistance, and evasion (SERE); surveillance; and communications. Upon completion of this course they are assigned to an operations team with Delta.

remote site at Fort Bragg. The Delta operators come from a mature military background, all NCOs and captains, minimum. The Force attracts most of its recruits from the ranks of the Rangers and Special Forces (SF), although others are considered according to the need of the unit. Having such outstanding individuals to draw upon, Delta is undisputedly the cream of the crop.

Constant preparation and cross training with other CT units, foreign and domestic, is ongoing and establishes a relationship of close cooperation within the community. This interactivity also provides the Delta operators with the opportunity to exchange information and lessons learned on tactics, techniques, and weapons, which could be employed in real-world operations. Even when they are not actively engaged in a CT mission, they may be in attendance as observers or advisers. Deltas are experts in Infil & Exfil, disguise, and surreptitious entry. These operators are the gurus of combat, whether armed with suppressed weapons, knives, or fighting hand to hand. They are the authority on CT and close-quarters battle (CQB)—the best of the best—period.

Their missions include, but are not limited to, Counter Terrorism, Hostage Rescue, Barricade Operations, Direct Action, and Unique Reconnaissance. They are organized and trained to conduct surgical strikes while carrying out their missions, and maintain a low profile. You need only look upon the beret, (worn by SF-qualified soldiers) which bears the flash and USASOC crest, which reads, *Sine Pari*—Without Equal!

Delta Karma

It is reported that a major league ball player once commented that he'd rather be lucky than good. Without question, Delta is certainly good, but it has not always been lucky. From Desert One to Somalia, this gathering of elite troops has gone all out, only to have the operation marred by the appearance of Mr. Murphy and his law.

During Operation Just Cause, the U.S. invasion of Panama in 1989, Delta was tasked with the rescue of Kurt Muse, an American citizen living in Panama who was disenchanted with the local government's corruption and its oppression of its people. Muse decided to tackle the problem head on. Using a strong radio transmitter, he and a handful of associates began overpowering the local radio stations and broadcasting anti-Noriega messages to the people of Panama.

At some point in time, the Central Intelligence Agency (CIA) became involved, and Muse now had an even more powerful transmitter. Muse and his people became bolder: They decided to break in on one of Gen. Manuel Noriega's official state speeches. Instead of hearing the general speak, the thousands of Panamanians heard a message from Muse titled "The Free Democratic People of Panama." When Noriega discovered what had happened, he was livid and mobilized his troops to find Muse and his team. Although hunted down by the Panamanian Defense Forces (PDF), they continued to broadcast for two months.

Muse's luck ran out when a member of the PDF returning from the United States recognized him from a flyer positioned at the international airport. This so-called "wanted poster" indicated that Muse was to be arrested on sight. Having identified Muse, the soldier contacted the civilian authorities, who arrested Muse on the spot. Muse would end up being sent to Modelo Prison, where he would spend the next nine months as Noreiga's prisoner. When news of Muse's capture reached the White House, President George H. Bush made the decision to rescue him and turned the details over to the military. The mission would be assigned to the 1st Special Forces Operational Detachment—Delta.

Initial planning for the rescue, named Operation Acid Gambit, began at Delta's complex at Fort Bragg, North Carolina. As the mission drew closer, the Delta operators moved down to Eglin Air Force Base, Florida, where a full-size mockup of the prison had been built. The mission called for the insertion of the assault team by helicopters from the 160th SOAR(A). Using four MH-6 "Little Birds," highly modified Hughes 500 light-attack helicopters, the Delta assault team would land on the roof of the prison and perform a dynamic entry by placing explosive charges on the doors. The team members would then negotiate down into the bowels of the prison, eliminating any hostile threats as they went. Once Muse had been located, the cell door would be blown using a small explosive charge and the team would bring him to the roof, where the awaiting helicopter would whisk him and his rescuers away to safety.

In support of this mission, a team of Delta snipers armed with .50 caliber sniper rifles would be positioned in the vicinity to remove any threat from outside guards. In addition to the snipers, there were two AH-6 "Little Birds." Working in conjunction with the SOAR(A) helicopters would be two AC-130H "Spectre" gunships from the 1st Special Operation Wing from Hurlburt Field, Florida. The Air Force assets had pre-assigned targets, as well as the assignment to be on hand to lend Close Air Support (CAS) to the rescue.

Just after midnight the two AH-6 helicopters began their gun run, raking the roofs of nearby buildings and launching rockets at the neighboring Comandancia. Operation Acid Gambit had begun. Having neutralized the guards outside the prison, the sniper team turned its heavy-caliber rifles toward the prison's generators. Within minutes the generator was destroyed and the building plunged into darkness.

Through the darkness of the prison the Delta team members worked their way toward Muse's cell using night-vision goggles (NVGs). Within minutes, Muse was released and on his way up to the roof—his first steps toward going home. Once on the roof, Muse was positioned inside the MH-6, with a Delta operator on each side of him. Six additional troops hopped on the outboard platforms and the "Little Bird" arched skyward. Any satisfaction Kurt Muse and the team were feeling would quickly be put on hold . . . enter Mr. Murphy. Looking through his NVGs, the pilot observed at the very front of the small helicopters a string of power lines blocking their egress. Trying to pull pitch, the heavily burdened helicopter promptly lost altitude and headed for the street below. Only the expertise and experience of the 160th pilots managed to keep the "Bird" in the air.

Now, flying just above the pavement, the "Night Stalker" pilot maneuvered his damaged craft with its charges between the buildings and away from the incoming fire of the Comandancia and prison. After a brief respite on the ground, the pilot managed to get the helicopter into the air again. Any elation was cut short, however, as the "Little Bird" was struck by a hail of bullets, causing it to crash onto the pavement below. Three men were injured in the crash and another wounded from gunfire. As the aircraft leaned to its side, Muse and his rescuers made a hasty exit. The remaining Delta team members moved Muse and the casualties to the refuge of a nearby apartment building. Muse asked for a weapon and one of the operators obliged, handing him a Colt .45 semi-automatic pistol. En route to the building, one of the Delta members fell as if he had been shot. Muse hit the ground next to the man. What at first appeared to have been a gunshot, however, was the result of the rotor blades from the helicopter clipping the operator's helmet. Once back on their feet, the two men joined the others in the relative safety of the apartment building.

Using an infrared strobe, the Delta team was able to identify its position to helicopters flying overhead. Moments later a U.S. Army Blackhawk overflew their position and wiggled its pods, indicating it had a fix on their position. The group's location was relayed to a U.S. Army patrol, and shortly thereafter an M-113 armored personnel carrier (APC) rumbled down the street to extract Muse, the wounded, and the balance of the rescue team. Although the APC did take gun-

fire as it headed toward the Canal Zone and then on to Howard Air Force Base, Kurt Muse was now secure and on his way home. Operation Acid Gambit had been a success! The combined efforts of Delta, the 160th SOAR(A) and AFSOC "Spectres" had successfully carried out the rescue of an American hostage from an enemy on foreign soil.

Desert Storm

Although experiencing a little bad luck with the downing of the MH-6 in Panama, the four wounded Delta operators recovered and returned to duty. The Force would not be so fortunate during the Persian Gulf War. On 21 February 1991, during Operation Desert Storm, the call came in for the urgent extraction of a Delta team requesting a medical evacuation. A MH-60L Blackhawk from Company C 1-160th SOAR(A), #251, responded to the call. The aircraft was immediately airborne and heading toward the extraction point. Probing deep into Iraqi territory at night, the pilots flew using their Night Vision Goggles, flying as low as 50 feet above the desert in order to evade the many anti-aircraft artillery (AAA) threats en route. Traveling at a speed of 120 knots through fog and low visibility, the pilots located and successfully extracted the wounded soldier and waiting team. With the team now safely aboard, the "Night Stalker" headed back to base and the medical facility. During this trip, however, Blackhawk #251 encountered a sandstorm and lost all visual reference to the ground. This resulted in the downing of the aircraft, its crew, and the team of Delta operators. Unfortunately, the outcome was the loss of all personnel on board.

Scud Hunting

One of the prime targets designated by Saddam Hussein was the country of Israel. If he could provoke Israel into the war, the delicate alliance between the United States and Arab coalition forces could easily be destroyed. The Arabs might fight alongside the Americans, but they could never allow themselves to be aligned with the Israelis. Therefore, all efforts were made to keep the Israelis out of the fighting. The Scud issue was no longer just a tactical concern; it had escalated into a priority strategic issue. The Scuds had to be located and destroyed. Since the Scuds were loaded on the combination mobile transport, erector, launcher (TEL) the Iraqis could move the missiles randomly, set them up, fire, and move out before coalition aircraft could locate and destroy them. At the beginning of

A Fast Attack Vehicle (FAV) prepares for a mission at King Fahad Airport, Saudi Arabia. Delta Force employed these light strike vehicles in its Scud-hunting missions. Loaded onto MH-47 helicopters of the 160th SOAR(A), they were inserted deep into Iraq to hunt down the elusive TEL and Scud missiles. *Author collection*

Desert Storm, members of the British SAS were in Iraq; their mission was to locate the elusive Scud missiles and call in coalition air strikes.

In February 1991 a Joint Special Operations Task Force (JSOTF) arrived in Saudi Arabia. With approximately 400 men, the JSOTF would include the 160th SOAR(A) and Delta Force. Working alongside the SAS in western Iraq, the Delta operators would join the Scud-hunting mission. As A-10 "Warthogs" scoured the desert below and F-15 "Eagles" and other coalition aircraft streaked across the skies, Delta would dash across the desert sand, all in search of the elusive TELs, Scuds, and their command and control elements.

While the SAS operated in the southern area known as "Scud Alley," Delta teams were assigned to the northern section in the area of the Tigris and Euphrates Rivers, referred to as "Scud Boulevard." Inserted by MH-47 helicopters of the 160th SOAR(A), the Delta teams would unload their FAVs and begin their mission. These highly mobile, agile, and speedy dune buggies enabled the operators to negotiate the sands and wadis of the Iraqi desert. The FAVs were heavily armed for a lightweight vehicle. With AT-4 anti-tank weapons, M-2 .50 caliber machine guns, and other assorted weaponry, they were certainly tigers on the prowl. The most lethal weapon they carried, however, would be the laser-aiming designators and radios. If the team located a missile, it could "light up" the target, and an attack aircraft would drop a smart bomb, which would lock on to the laser and the target.

Two of the military elements that dealt with the Israelis' tolerance of the Scud missile attacks during the Gulf War were, first, the placement of Patriot missiles in Israel to counter the Scud attacks, and second, the commitment of the SAS and Delta Force missions. While operational accounts may differ on the actual "Scud Kills" accredited to the British and U.S. Special Forces, it can clearly be stated the "Great Scud Hunt" was a strategic success. General Schwarzkopf would later comment that the combined efforts of the SAS and Special Forces (Delta) concerning the Scuds were instrumental in keeping Israel out of the war.

Delta almost got the "go" call for a hostage rescue during Operation Desert Storm. As Iraqi armor was pouring over the border into Kuwait, planers at JSOC were immediately working on possible rescue scenarios to extract hostages from the embassy or other locations in Kuwait, should the need arise. Saddam Hussein was pushing the SOF into just such a position when he took many of the Kuwaitis and foreign nationals and held them hostage during the opening days of the war. He planned to use them as human shields should the U.S.-led coalition press a ground war. Such a thought was intolerable to the U.S. government, and it put plans into place to rescue the hostages. This mission was called Operation Pacific Wind, and Delta was tasked with the assignment.

Using actual blueprints and intelligence gathered from various sources, the government built a mockup of the embassy at a remote site on Eglin AFB, Florida. Here the Delta operators and aircrews of the 160th SOAR(A) practiced their approach, assault, and rescue of the hostages. With Kuwait city located so close to the Gulf and the American forces, a hostage rescue seemed to be a feasible plan and well within the grasp and capabilities of Delta. General Schwarzkopf was concerned that, if the mission failed, it could result in all-out war with the Iraqis, and he was not ready to commit his forces at this time. Operation Pacific Wind was therefore put on hold. The Delta teams were poised for what would be their

Delta Force was tasked with an assortment of assignments during Desert Storm. Here Delta operators provide security for the commander-in-chief (CinC) U.S. Central Command Gen. Norman H. Schwarzkopf. While not as glamorous a duty as speeding around the desert in an FAV, it was a job that would not be trusted to anyone but Delta operators. Their experience in dealing with a terrorist threat; their keen sense of observation, and their lethality made them the perfect choice to safeguard "The Bear." *Defense Visual Information Center*

delta force missions

Delta operators have been directly or indirectly involved in the following:

1979	Worked with the FBI at the Pan-American Games in Puerto Rico.
1980	Initiated Operation Eagle Claw, Iran; hostage rescue.
1981	Called to take down terrorists who had hijacked an Indonesian airplane in Bangkok.
1981	Possible POW rescue in Laos.
1981	Sent an intelligence team to Italy to aid in the search for kidnapped Brig. Gen. James Dozier.
1981	Traveled to Honduras to act as security guards for an intelligence meeting regarding Nicaragua.
1983	Deployed along with other SOF units to Grenada during Operation Urgent Fury.
1983	Deployed to Beirut.
1984	Requested to react to the hijacking of a Kuwaiti airliner; logistics problems, however, caused Delta not to be deployed.
1984	Suspected to have participated in Operation Manta in Libya. French special forces and Delta inserted small teams to plant surveillance equipment around terrorist training camps.
1984	Worked with LAPD and SWAT teams to provide security at Olympic Games in Los Angeles.
1985	Loaded up and headed to Algiers after TWA Flight 847 hijacking by Shiite extremists. The Algerian government refused Delta permission to mount a rescue operation in the country.
1985	Placed on full alert, along with SEAL team, when the Italian ship *S.S. Achille Lauro*, with about 400 hostages—a large number of them American—was hijacked by four terrorists.
1986	Assisted with security during the rededication of the Statue of Liberty Centennial celebration in New York.
1987	Called up to assist the FBI with rioting prisoners in the federal penitentiary in Atlanta.
1989	Deployed when Special Forces soldiers were trapped in San Salvador; Special Forces accomplished Evasion and Escape (E&E), however, before operators arrived.
1989	Sent in to rescue U.S. nationals during army coup in the Philippines.
1989	Operation Just Cause, Panama. The rescue of Kurt Muse (Operation Acid Gambit) and apprehension of Gen. Manuel Noriega (Operation Nifty Package).

1990	Operation Desert Storm, Iraq. Delta deployed to perform DA missions, Scud hunting, and also served as bodyguards to the CinC, Gen. Norman H. Schwarzkopf.
1990	Operation Pacific Wind, readied for the rescue of U.S. citizens from the U.S. Embassy in Kuwaiti. Mission was not given a "go."
1993	1st SFOD-D summoned to Waco, Texas. Delta Force operators present as advisers to the FBI.
1993	Task Force Ranger; Somalia. Delta mission to capture warlord Aideed; resulted in 18 friendly KIAs, including six Delta operators.
1993	Delta intelligence team worked with Colombians in tracking down Pablo Escobar.
1994	Took part in Operation Uphold Democracy in Haiti.
1996	Put on alert in case of terrorist attack at the Olympic Games in Atlanta.
1997	Sent to Lima, Peru, along with British SAS when terrorists captured the Japanese Ambassador's residence.
1998	Deployed in Kosovo, along with British SAS and other NATO special operations units, in support of Operation Allied Force.

1998	U.S. officials acknowledge that U.S. and U.K. special operations units have been training for "snatch" operations in preparation for a possible mission to apprehend Serbian president Slobodan Milosevic.
1998	U.S. embassies in Kenya and Tanzania are bombed. Delta Force is given mission to capture or neutralize Osama Bin Laden. Mission is planned; however, Delta does not deploy, having concern over reliability of intelligence.
1999	Deployed operators to assist in security during the World Trade Organization meeting, Seattle, Washington.
1999	Placed on alert during concern over terrorist threat during the Millennium.
2001	Team prepared for hostage-rescue mission of U.S. oil workers in Ecuador. State Department does not deploy.
2001	Placed on high alert after terrorists attack World Trade Center in New York City and The Pentagon in Washington, D.C.
2001	Deployed to Afghanistan.
2002	Activated in terrorist hunt.

One of the missions of Delta Force is Direct Action (DA). These missions include, but are not limited to, seizure, destroying, capture of enemy personnel, or any action inflicting damage on enemy personnel or material. DA may include the recovery of sensitive items or personnel, for example, hostage rescue. Delta is highly trained and may employ raids, ambushes, and other small-unit tactics in the pursuit of these mission goals. Delta operators may employ standoff weapons, such as a sniper team or a team "Lasing" a target for terminal guidance ordnance (TGO), i.e. precision guided "smart bombs." C&C centers are always high-priority targets as seen here during the assault and securing of a radar site.

largest mission since Operation Eagle Claw and waited for orders to deploy to the Gulf. In December 1990, Hussein reversed his position and released the hostages without incident. Delta Force stood down and Operation Pacific Wind was shelved.

A less challenging task, but nonetheless an important one, came in the assignment of Delta operators to be personal bodyguards for the CinC, Gen. Norman H. Schwarzkopf.

Task Force Ranger

The problem with high-risk missions is the high probability of casualties. The sensitivity of high-risk mission means you need to send in your best people. When such missions require stealth, speed, and violence of action, they require the deployment of Delta. Casualties are an occupational hazard in these types of endeavors. If you are commanding an infantry company and you suffer four or five wounded, it might be distressing, but you are still operational however, considering a Delta team operates with a four-man element, if you experience two wounded, you have just depleted your force by 50 percent!

A half a world away from Fort Bragg, North Carolina, on the eastern coast of Africa, the United States entered into Operation Restore Hope in Somalia in the spring of 1992, as a humanitarian operation. The mission would encompass the securing of major airports and seaports, key installations, and food-distribution points. The U.S. military involvements included security for convoys, relief operations, and consequently assisting U.N. and nongovernmental organizations to provide humanitarian relief in Somalia under U.N. auspices. United Nations Operations in Somalia, or UNOSOM I had not brought the expected political results. UNOSOM II was a U.N. peacekeeping mission providing humanitarian and relief activities, led by U.S. Navy Adm. Jonathan Howe as Special Representative of the Secretary General, with Turkish Lt. Gen. Cevik Bir as force commander of the U.N. multinational force.

Clan warlords continually ambushed the convoys, stole the food, and caused havoc throughout the area. The stepped-up attacks by the Gen. Mohammed Farad Aideed, the main warlord, caused Les Aspin, the Secretary of Defense in August 1993, to order the deployment of a JSOTF to support the U.S. mission in Somalia. The U.N. Security Council Resolution 837, which set the mandate for Task Force Ranger (TFR), was largely drafted by the United States. The task force (TF) mission was to capture Aideed and his lieutenants and turn them over to the UNOSOM II forces.

On 28 August 1993, the JSOTF arrived in Somalia to begin its assignment. The task force, numbering almost 400 special operations personnel, would include U.S. Army Rangers, helicopters from the 160th SOAR(A), U.S. Air Force Special Tactics Teams, and a complement of U.S. Navy SEALs and Delta Force members. Maj. Gen. William Garrison commanded TFR, reporting directly to General Hoar at Central Command (CENTCOM); JSOTF was always under U.S. command. It would be here, in the city of Mogadishu, Somalia, in the fall of 1993 that the United States would enter into the single most deadly firefight since the Vietnam War.

On 3 October 1993, members of TFR conducted a daylight raid on an enemy stronghold deep in militia-held Mogadishu. Operators of 1st Special Force Operational Detachment–Delta were tasked to capture two of Aideed's lieutenants. According to Intelligence Support Activity (ISA) sources, these aides were in the building a block away from the Olympic Hotel. This was in the Bakara area, one of the most dangerous parts of the city. Helicopters from the 160th SOAR(A) launched from the TFR compound at Mogadishu airport at 1532 hours, with a ground convoy moving out shortly thereafter. Aircraft heading

for the target included two MH-6 "Little Birds" with the lead Delta teams; eight Blackhawks carrying the additional Delta assaulters (members of the 75th Ranger Battalion); a Combat Search And Rescue (CSAR) helicopter; and finally the Command and Control (C&C) helicopter.

At 1542 hours the lead element of Delta landed in front of the target building. At the same time the Rangers were fast roping at four separate intersections surrounding the designated site. This cordon of Rangers would ensure no one got into or out of Delta's Area of Operations (AO). Doing what they do best, the Delta team members began their assault. Placing explosive charges, they breached the outer gate and door, allowing swift entrance into the building. Working their way through the smoke and dust, the assault team members negotiated their way to the objective and captured the individuals. The snatch-and-grab was accomplished in approximately 15 minutes, and with their prisoners in hand they called for extraction. The egress would be via Humvees of the ground convoy, which was en route to evacuate the prisoners and the assault force.

Upon the arrival of the ground convoy, the Delta assault team began loading the prisoners into the Humvees for the trip back to the TF compound. During the loading, an MH-60 Blackhawk was shot down by a rocket-propelled grenade (RPG) and crashed three blocks from the target location. The helicopter was carrying a portion of the Delta assault force; two of the operators were killed on impact. Without delay, a six-man element of the Ranger blocking force, in addition to an MH-6 assault helicopter and an MH-60 carrying a 15-man CSAR teams headed for the crash site. The MH-6 crew got there first, and, amid a firefight, evacuated two wounded soldiers to a military field hospital. By this time the six-man blocking element arrived, followed by the CSAR helicopter. As the last two members of the CSAR slid down the fast ropes, an RPG hit their helicopter. The pilot started to take off; however, seeing he still had people on the "rope," he steadied the helicopter, allowing the last two to reach the ground safely. He then headed back to the airport. Leaving that helicopter, the crew then headed back to the fighting.

No sooner had they secured the MH-60 than ground fire struck two more MH-60s, with one crashing less than a mile to the south of the first crash site. Under severe fire from machine guns and RPGs, the force grouped together and established a perimeter inside buildings to treat their wounded and wait for extraction. A Somali mob overran this second site and, despite courageous resistance, killed everyone except

Two Delta operators, MSG Gary Ivan Gordon and SFC Randall D. Shughart, were awarded Medals of Honor for their actions in Somalia. This awarding of the MOH would be the first since the Vietnam War; also noteworthy is the fact that both of the medals were awarded to snipers. Official transcripts of their citations are listed below. Both MOHs were awarded posthumously.

Master Sergeant Gary I. Gordon

"Rank and organization: Master Sergeant, U.S. Army. Place and date: 3 October 1993, Mogadishu, Somalia. Born: Lincoln, Maine. Citation: Master Sergeant Gordon, United States Army, distinguished himself by actions above and beyond the call of duty on 3 October 1993, while serving as Sniper Team Leader, United States Army Special Operations Command with Task Force Ranger in Mogadishu, Somalia.

"Master Sergeant Gordon's sniper team provided precision fires from the lead helicopter during an assault and at two helicopter crash sites, while subjected to intense automatic weapons and rocket-propelled grenade fires. When Master Sergeant Gordon learned that ground forces were not immediately available to secure the second crash site, he and another sniper unhesitatingly volunteered to be inserted to protect the four critically wounded personnel, despite being well aware of the growing number of enemy personnel closing in on the site.

"After his third request to be inserted, Master Sergeant Gordon received permission to perform his volunteer mission. When debris and enemy ground fires at the site caused them to abort the first attempt, Master Sergeant Gordon was inserted one hundred meters south of the crash site. Equipped with only his sniper rifle and a pistol, Master Sergeant Gordon and his fellow sniper, while under intense small arms fire from the enemy, fought their way through a dense maze of shanties and shacks to reach the critically injured crew members. Master Sergeant Gordon immediately pulled the pilot and the other crew members from the aircraft, establishing a perimeter which placed him and his fellow sniper in the most vulnerable position.

"Master Sergeant Gordon used his long-range rifle and sidearm to kill an undetermined number of attackers until he depleted his ammunition. Master Sergeant Gordon then went back to the wreckage, recovering some of the crew's weapons and ammunition. Despite the fact that he was critically low on ammunition, he provided some of it to the dazed pilot and then radioed for help. Master Sergeant Gordon continued to travel the perimeter, protecting the downed crew. After his team member was fatally wounded and his own rifle ammunition exhausted, Master Sergeant Gordon returned to the wreckage, recovering a rifle with the last five rounds of ammunition and gave it to the pilot with the words, "good luck." Then, armed only with his pistol, Master Sergeant Gordon continued to fight until he was fatally wounded. His actions saved the pilot's life. Master Sergeant Gordon's extraordinary heroism and devotion to duty were in keeping with the highest standards of military service and reflect great credit upon him, his unit and the United States Army."

Sergeant First Class Randall D. Shughart

"Rank and organization: Sergeant First Class, U.S. Army. Place and date: 3 October 1993, Mogadishu, Somalia. Born: Newville, Pennsylvania. Citation: Sergeant First Class Shughart, United States Army, distinguished himself by actions above and beyond the call of duty on 3 October 1993, while serving as a Sniper Team Member, United States Army Special Operations Command with Task Force Ranger in Mogadishu, Somalia.

"Sergeant First Class Shughart provided precision sniper fire from the lead helicopter during an assault on a building and at two helicopter crash sites, while subjected to intense automatic weapons and rocket-propelled grenade fires. While providing critical suppressive fires at the second crash site, Sergeant First Class Shughart and his team leader learned that ground forces were not immediately available to secure the site. Sergeant First Class Shughart and his team leader unhesitatingly volunteered to be inserted to protect the four critically wounded personnel, despite being well aware of the growing number of enemy personnel closing in on the site.

"After their third request to be inserted, Sergeant First Class Shughart and his team leader received permission to perform this volunteer mission. When debris and enemy ground fires at the site caused them to abort the first attempt, Sergeant First Class Shughart and his team leader were inserted one hundred meters south of the crash site. Equipped with only his sniper rifle and a pistol, Sergeant First Class Shughart and his team leader, while under intense small arms fire from the enemy, fought their way through a dense maze of shanties and shacks to reach the critically injured crewmembers. Sergeant First Class Shughart pulled the pilot and the other crew members from the aircraft, establishing a perimeter, which placed him and his fellow sniper in the most vulnerable position.

"Sergeant First Class Shughart used his long range rifle and side arm to kill an undetermined number of attackers while traveling the perimeter, protecting the downed crew. Sergeant First Class Shughart continued his protective fire until he depleted his ammunition and was fatally wounded. His actions saved the pilot's life. Sergeant First Class Shughart's extraordinary heroism and devotion to duty were in keeping with the highest standards of military service and reflect great credit upon him, his unit and the United States Army."

the pilot, who was taken prisoner. Two of the defenders at the crash site were Delta snipers, MSG Gary Gordon and SFC Randall Shughart. The two were later posthumously awarded the Medal of Honor for their actions at the crash site. The other 160th Blackhawk was hit broadside by an RPG, but its crew members managed to evade to the new port area, while they did a controlled crash landing. The mission now turned from what had become a simple assault to what would be a fight for the survival of TFR.

Roadblocks and heavy gunfire along the narrow streets of Mogadishu would necessitate the detouring of the second convoy to the west where it came in contact with the first convoy. Upon meeting, the second group loaded casualties onto its vehicles and escorted the first convoy back to base. Meanwhile, the mission's quick reaction force (QRF), a company of the 10th Mountain Division in support of UNOSOM II, also tried to reach the second crash site. The QRF also was trapped by Somali fire and required fire support from two AH-6 helicopters before it could break contact and return to the airport.

During the evening, the TFR soldiers at the first crash site were resupplied from a helicopter. Finally at 0166 hours on 4 October reinforcements of a reconstituted QRF consisting of Rangers, 10th Mountain Division soldiers, SEALs, and Malaysian APCs finally arrived at the downed helicopter. Despite the fact that they were taking fire from small arms and RPGs throughout the night, the combined force worked until dawn to free the pilot's body.

The world is urbanizing, the population is becoming more and more dense, and Delta operators must be able to perform in that environment conducting hostage rescues, CT operations, direct action missions, raids, and surgical strikes. When National Command Authority (NCA) commits Delta Force it expects soldiers that can apply lethal force with a high degree of precision. These lessons were learned at a costly price in October 1993 when U.S. SOF units were engaged in a firefight for their lives on the streets of Mogadishu, Somalia. *DoD*

With the casualties loaded onto the APCs, the armored personnel carriers provided cover as the remainder of the force headed out on foot. The Somalis fired sporadic small-arms fire and RPGs at the convoy, inflicting only minor wounds. As the convoy maneuvered through the gauntlet of the Mogadishu maze, AH-6 gunships raked the cross streets with fire to support the convoy's movement. By 0630 the main force of the convoy had arrived at the Pakistani Stadium; here emergency treatment was given to the wounded, and all personnel were prepared for movement to the hospital or the back to the TF compound at the airfield.

UNOSOM II was considered successful in that it accomplished, with the introduction of a strong military force, the opening up of transportation routes, enabled the provision of humanitarian and relief supplies, and stabilized the situation. During August and September the Task Force would run six missions into Mogadishu. These missions were conducted during both the day and at night; all were tactically successful. In total, TFR

conducted seven raids on the warlord, including the mission of 3 October; they had successfully captured 23 of Aideed's top men—nearly his entire high command. Task force members had to operate in an especially challenging environment, requiring the hallmarks of special operations soldiers: the abilities to adapt, overcome, improvise, and exhibit sound judgment. The TF had more than held its own against a numerically superior enemy that was battled-hardened from years of civil war and experience in urban fighting.

Although TFR suffered a high percentage of casualties (with little or no support,) dwindling supplies, and facing a force hundreds of times greater in numbers, Task Force Rangers held their ground for more than 18 hours, maintained control of their prisoners, killed an estimated 300, and wounded more than 700. However, it came at a very high cost to Delta and the supporting U.S. forces. Its outcome would find 18 soldiers of TFR killed, and it would be the worst combat disaster for Delta Force, resulting in the loss of six Delta operators.

(left) Outfitted with Night Vision Goggles (NVGs) and armed with the latest weapons and IR devices, Delta Force owns the night. Whether inserting covertly into the desert of Iraq or hunting in the mountains of Afghanistan, the operators are equipped to carry out their mission.

(below) The silence of the night is broken as the demolition charge rips through a target during a training mission. Whether extracting a hostage or performing a Direct Action (DA) mission such as pictured here, nothing is left to chance. Operations are planned, rehearsed, critiqued, and rehearsed again. Success in Delta operations comes by "sweating the small stuff."

After Action Report (AAR)

The fact that 1st Special Forces Operational Detachment–Delta has not experienced the wide-reaching limelight contributes to the reality: Most of the group's missions are conducted with the utmost secrecy. The successes of Delta are achieved when, in actuality, no one even knows they were onsite. Their operations have lacked the fanfare of Entebbe or Princess Gate, and that is just fine with these quiet professionals. In truth, Delta has been deployed on numerous missions, and its involvement, whether direct, indirect, or in an advisory capacity, has made the difference for a hostage—that difference between filling a body bag and going home to family.

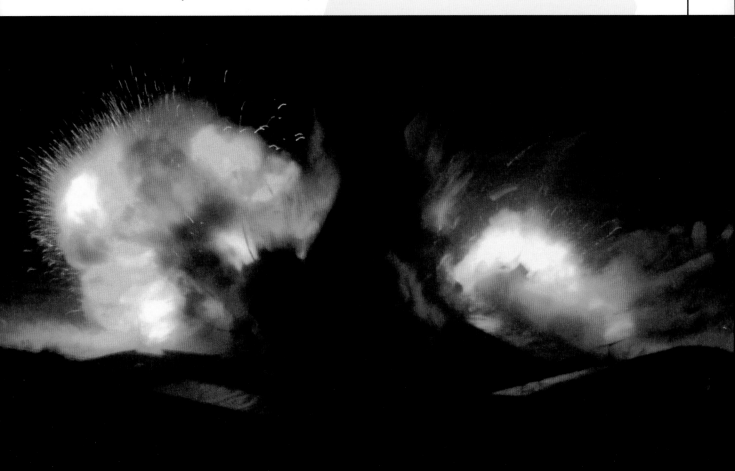

M4A1 Carbine

Numerous accessories can be added to a weapon with the RIS. This M4A1 carbine is equipped with Aimpoint Red Dot sight, AN/PEQ-4 IR Laser pointer, Visible "white" Light, and M203, 40mm grenade launcher. The shooter is wearing a helmet by Gallet, Oakley Tactical goggles, and an Eagle Assault Vest. *Department of Defense*

M4A1 Carbine

In 1994 the USSOCOM adopted the M4 carbine, replacing the M16A2, M3 "Grease Gun," and selected M9 semiautomatic pistols. When selecting a weapon, the operators will use a mix of criteria, including accuracy, range, size, weight, weight of ammo, availability of ammo, ammo capacity, rate of fire, ease of concealment, ease of maintenance, and penetrating power. As a basic-issue weapon for a special operations soldier, the M4 is probably a better choice based on accuracy, range, availability of ammo, ease of maintenance, and penetrating power. Although the operators are given wide latitude in the selection of primary and secondary weapons, the M4A1 is the new weapon of choice in the CQB/CT role of the Delta shooter. With the advent of terrorists and other hostiles employing body armor and bulletproof vests, it was paramount that CQB/CT operations migrated from the 9mm rounds to the higher penetration capabilities of the 5.56mm ammunition. According to informed sources, the Colt M4A1 is currently the official issue and primary weapon in use in Delta Force.

The M4A1 from Colt Manufacturing Company of Connecticut is a smaller, compact version of the full-sized M16A2 rifle. This weapon was designed specifically for the U.S. SOF. The main difference between the standard M4 and the M4A1 is that the fire selector for the M4 can be set for semi or three-round burst, while the M4A1 has a fire selection for semi- and full-automatic operation. The M4A1 is designed for speed of action and lightweight requirements, as is often the case for Delta weapons. The barrel has been redesigned to a shortened 14.5 inches, which reduces the weight, while maintaining its effectiveness for quick-handling field operations. The retractable buttstock has four intermediate stops, allowing versatility in CQB without compromising shooting capabilities.

The M4A1 has a rifling twist of 1 in 7 inches, which makes it compatible with the full range of 5.56mm ammunitions. Its sighting system contains dual apertures, allowing for 0–200 meters and a smaller opening for engaging targets at a longer range of 500–600 meters. Selective fire controls for the M4 have eliminated the three-round burst, replacing it with safe semi-automatic and full-automatic fire.

In addition to the CQB capabilities of the carbine, the M4A1 also provides the necessary firepower when targets must be engaged at greater ranges. In Operation Desert Storm, certain elements were equipped with some suppressed 9mm rifles while performing Special Reconnaissance (SR) missions. When one of the teams was compromised and facing a rush of oncoming Iraqi soldiers and local nomads, it would be the M16 and carbines laying down a hail of 5.56mm rounds out to 400–600 meters, allowing the team the extra edge they needed to extract from a bad situation. The same line of reasoning holds fast from the Somali experience. The M16 carbine proved to be more durable and versatile, and the 5.56mm ammunition more lethal than the 9mm pistol round.

The lineage of the M4A1 goes back almost five decades to the mid-1950s when the U.S. military sought a weapon to replace the heavy M14 battle rifle. In 1959 that weapon, the M16 rifle, was born. A product of Eugene Stoner, this lightweight assault weapon was viewed with apprehension when first introduced. Soldiers used to the heavy M1 and M14 rifles often referred to it as "the toy gun." As the war continued, other modifications of the M16 series were developed and the XM177E1 was introduced to the U.S. troops. This shortened version of the M16, with a collapsible stock and various barrel lengths, was often referred to as the CAR-15. The CAR-15 saw service with the SEALs, LRRPs, SOG, and other special operations soldiers. This carbine version of the M16 laid the groundwork for the Colt M4/M4A1 carbine in use today, which has evolved into the weapon of choice for today's special operations forces in general and Delta Force operators in particular.

M4A1 specs

Caliber: 5.56mm
Weight: 5.56 pounds (without magazine), 6.65 pounds (with loaded magazine-30 rounds)
Length: 33.0 inches (stock extended), 29.8 inches (stock retracted)
Barrel Length: 14.5 inches
Muzzle Velocity: 3,020 ft/sec (M193), 2,900 ft/sec (M844NATO)
Muzzle Energy: 1,113 ft-lbs (M193), 1,213 ft-lbs (MM855 NATO)
Maximum Effective Range: 393 yards (M193), 656 yards (M855/SS109 NATO)
Cyclic Rate of Fire: 700–950 rpm
Fire Selection: Semi/Full Automatic

Special Operations Peculiar Modification (SOPMOD) M4A1 Accessory Kit

The M4A1 carbine is a most capable and deadly weapon, suitable to any Delta mission. USASOC wanted to make the weapon even more effective, whether for close-in engagements or long-range targets. To accomplish this, USSOCOM and the Naval Surface Warfare Center's Crane Division developed the SOPMOD Kit. Introduced in 1994 along with the M4 carbine, the SOPMOD kit, is issued to all U.S. Special Operations Forces to expand the capabilities and operation of the M4A1 carbine.

The SOPMOD accessory kit consists of numerous components that may be attached directly onto the M4A1 carbine or attached to the Rail Interface System (RIS). These various accessories give the operator the flexibility to choose the appropriate optics, lasers, lights, and more, dependent on mission parameters. The SOPMOD kit is constantly being evaluated, and research is ongoing to further enhance the operability, functionality, and lethality of the M4A1 carbine. Currently, the kit is in Block 1 of a three-phase upgrade and modification program. Delta operators will also use other military and commercial off the shelf (COTS) modifications to enhance the M4A1 and the SOPMOD kit, dependent on mission parameters.

SOPMOD M4 Accessory Kit

- Carrying Handle/Sight
- ACOG Reflex 0-300m Range
- ACOG 4X Scope 0-600m Range
- Visible Laser 0-300m Range
- AN/PEQ-2 IR Pointer/Illuminator 0-600m Range
- Backup Iron Sight 0-300m Range
- Rail Interface System (RIS)
- M4A1 Carbine (5.56 mm NATO)
- Forward HandGrip
- QD Sound Suppressor 30 dB Reduction
- Visible Light 9 Volt
- M203 Grenade Launcher with QD Mount
- Modified M203 Leaf Sight

Special Operations Peculiar Modification to the M4 Carbine (SOPMOD M4) Accessory Kit

Program Objective: To provide Special Operations Forces the ability to adapt the M4A1 Carbine to increase its operational effectiveness through improved target recognition, acquisition, and hit quality during day and night from Close Quarters to 500 meters.

Program Sponsors: United States Special Operations Command

Program Manager: Crane Division, Naval Surface Warfare Center

SOPMOD M4 Website: http://ammo-eng.crane.navy.mil/408html/sopmod3.htm

The M4A1 shown here has been modified with the Special Operations Peculiar Modification (SOPMOD) accessory kit. The Rail Interface System, or RIS, allows the attachment of numerous aiming devices and accessories depending on the mission. This M4A1 has been modified with a Trijicon ACOG (Advanced Combat Optical Gunsight) 4x32 scope; on the handgrip is an AN/PEQ-2 Infrared Target Pointer/Illuminator/Aiming Laser (ITPIAL). The PEQ-2 emits a laser beam for precise aiming of the weapon. It may also be used for lasing target for the delivery of smart bombs. Finally, attached to the barrel is a Quick Attach/Detach (QAD) Sound Suppressor. With the suppressor attached, the muzzle blast, flash, and sound are significantly reduced. *Department of Defense*

1995–2001 M4A1 + SOPMOD Block 1

The M4A1 is the carbine version of the M16A2 assault rifle, but it is more compact, incorporating a collapsible stock, 14.5-inch barrel and a detachable carrying handle which, when removed, reveals a Weaver-type rail for mounting SOPMOD accessories. The original M4/M16A2 carbine featured a safe semi- and three-round-burst fire selector. The modified M4A1 removed the three-round-burst option and replaced it with full automatic selection. According to the reports from the Army's Picatinny Arsenal, " . . . the M4A1 is three times more reliable than called for in the original specifications." It can be even better, however, so the folks at SOCOM, Crane, and Picatinny—as well as numerous suppliers and manufactures—are constantly working on improving this premier special operations weapon.

(above) The primary rifle in use with Delta is the Colt M4A1 carbine. This shortened version of the M16A2 rifle features a collapsible stock, a flat top upper receiver with an accessory rail, and a detachable handle/rear aperture sight assembly. The M4A1 has a fire selection for semi- and fully-automatic operation. Seen here is a "vanilla" M4A1, sans SOPMOD accessories.

(top right) Here is a good shot of a "tricked out" M4. It is fitted with the sound suppressor, the AN/PEQ-2 ITPIAL and Trijicon ACOG, 4X sight. With a wide assortment of accessories the M4A1, SOPMOD carbine can adapt to any mission profile.

Rail Interface System (RIS)

The Rail Interface system (RIS) is a notched-rail system, which replaces the front hand guards on the M4A1 receiver. This rail system is located on the top, bottom, and sides of the barrel, facilitating the attaching of SOPMOD kit components on any of the four sides. The notches are numbered, making it possible to attach, and reattach the various components at the same position each time it is mounted. Optical sights and Night Vision Devices (NVD) can be mounted on the top, while top and side rails would be the choice for positioning laser-aiming devices or lights. The bottom of the RIS normally will accommodate the vertical grip and/or lights. When no accessories are mounted to the RIS, plastic hand guards are emplaced to cover and protect the unused portions of the rail.

ACOG (Advance Combat Optical Gunsight)

The ACOG manufactured by Trijicon is the Day Optical Scope for the SOPMOD kit. The ACOG is a four-power telescopic sight including a ballistic compensating reticle. Employing this reticle provides increased capability to direct, identify, and hit targets to the maximum effective range of the M4A1 carbine (600 meters). As a backup,

the ACOG is equipped with an iron sight for rapid Close Range Engagement (CRE). Both the front iron sight and the scope reticle provide target recognition and standoff attack advantage while retaining a close-quarter capability equivalent to the standard iron sights.

A SOPMOD refinement would combine a 4X scope with CQB capabilities. The Trijicon ACOG BAC 4x32 scope is one of the offerings to meet these requirements. The operator uses a red dot for CQB and the 4X for distance shots. The BAC stands for Bindon Aiming Concept: keeping both eyes open, the operator looks through the sight with one eye while concentrating on the target with the other eye. The brain automatically merges the two images. The Aimpoint COMP-M and the EOTech HDS sights also use this concept.

Trijicon ACOG provides increased hit potential in all lighting conditions. The exterior of the ACOG is a forged aluminum body (aircraft-strength 7075 alloy). The ACOG has internally adjustable, compact telescopic sights that use tritium illuminated reticles for target acquisition in all light conditions. U.S. Special Operations Command chose the ACOG 4x32 model for the SOPMOD kit.

A Trijicon ACOG 4x32 scope mounted on an M4A1. The ACOG is a 4X telescopic sight including a ballistic compensating reticle. Employing this reticle provides increased capability to direct, identify, and hit target to the maximum effective range of the M4A1 carbine (600 meters).

AN/PEQ-2 Infrared Illuminator/Aiming Laser

The ITPIAL is a dual-beam IR laser device used handheld or weapon mounted. The unit has seven modes of operation for aiming light and pointer/illuminator functioning individually or in combination, as well as high and low in aiming light power. The unit is waterproof down 2 atmospheres. The AN/PEQ-2, or "Pac2," as it is called, can be utilized to "paint" a target with the laser for the direction of Terminal Guided Ordnance, that is, "Smart Bombs."

The AN/PEQ-2 Infrared Target Pointer/ Illuminator/Aiming Laser (ITPIAL) allows the M4A1 to be effectively employed to 300 meters with standard-issue NVGs or a weapon-mounted NVD, that is, an AN/PVS-14. The IR illuminator broadens the capabilities of the NVGs in buildings, tunnels, jungle, overcast conditions, and other low-light conditions in which starlight alone would not be sufficient to support night vision. It also allows visibility in areas normally in shadow. At close range, a neutral density filter is used to eliminate flare around the aiming laser for improving the view of the target, for identification, and for precision aiming. This combination provides the operator with a decisive advantage over an opposing force with little or no night-vision capability. One captain commented, "When using a PEQ-2 on an M4 and PVS-7s, it is like the hand of God reaching out and taking out an individual."

Reflex Sight

The Trijicon Reflex Sight is a reflex collimator sight designed for Close-Quarters Battle (CQB). The Reflex Sight provides a fast method of acquiring and hitting close still and moving targets, as well as engaging targets while the marksman himself is moving. The sight employs a tritium-illuminated dot usable for low-light and nighttime. Effective out to 300 meters, the Reflex Sight is optimized for speed and accuracy in close-range engagements (<50 meters) and close combat (<200 meters), providing the operator a heads-up fire control during both day and night and with night vision equipment. The Reflex Sight can be used with either night-vision goggles or in combination with a night-vision monocular such as the AN/PVS-14; this arrangement provides a lightweight day/night capability without having to re-zero during the transition between day and night sights.

The Trijicon Reflex Sight is a reflex collimator sight designed for CQB. The reflex sight features an amber reticle that adjusts accordingly, glowing more or less brightly dependent on the ambient light conditions. One of the benefits of the Trijicon Reflex is that it can operate without batteries.

(below) The AN/PEQ-2 ITPIAL allows the M4A1 to be effectively employed to 300 meters with standard-issue night-vision goggles (NVG) or a weapon-mounted night-vision device, that is, an AN/PVS-14. One shooter commented, when the weapon is in this configuration, "it is like the hand of God reaching out and taking out the bad guy."

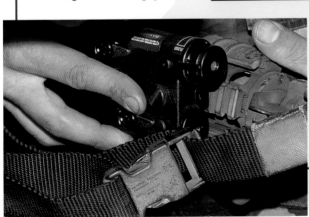

(above) This view through night-vision equipment demonstrates the capability of an AN/PEQ-2 attached to the M4A1. You can see the IR laser beam directed onto the target. There is a saying, "Do not fear the night. Fear what *hunts* in the night." Without a doubt, Delta operators are at home in the darkness.

Visible Light Illuminator

The Visible Light Illuminator (VLI) provides white light to facilitate moving inside dark buildings, bunkers, tunnels, and the like. The white light is useful for searching for and identifying the target. It has a dual-battery capability, meaning three three-volt lithium DL 123 batteries or six 1.5-volt AA batteries can power it. The Visible Light Illuminator is most useful in Military Operations Other Than War or Low Intensity Conflicts, when search and clear operations may be complicated by tripwires, booby traps, and non-combatants, and the danger of revealing your position is offset by the need for better vision than night-vision goggles (NVG) offer. The intense white light can overwhelm an opponent in CQB, giving the operator momentary advantage. An infrared (IR) filter can be attached to provide short-range illumination (50 meters) when using night vision equipment. This red filter also reduces glare in smoky environments and reduces impact on the operator's night vision.

The Forward or Vertical Handgrip attaches to the bottom of the RIS. In this configuration it provides added support, giving the operator a more stable firing platform. It can also serve as a monopod in a fixed shooting position.

Visible Laser AN/PEQ-5

The AN/PEQ-5, as the name implies, is a Visible Laser (VL) that attaches to the RIS and provides a close-range visible laser-aiming beam. The VL can be used at close range in a lighted building, in darkness with the Visible Light Illuminator, or at night with night-vision equipment. It is used primarily in CQB/CRE where it provides a fast and accurate means of aiming the weapon. It is especially valuable when the operator is wearing a protective mask, firing from an awkward position, or firing from behind cover and around corners. It permits the shooter to focus all his attention on the target while being able to accurately direct the point of impact. Since it is visible, it also provides a non-lethal show of force that can intimidate hostile personnel, that is, letting the "bad guys" know you have them in your sights.

Mini Night Vision Sight (MNVS)

The MNVS is a lightweight, compact night-vision sight that provides the operator with the capability to locate, identify, and engage targets from 20 to 300 meters. The MNVS features a wide field of view, magnified night-vision image, illuminated reticle, and is adjustable for windage/elevation. It can be hand held, or mounted on the weapons or helmet.

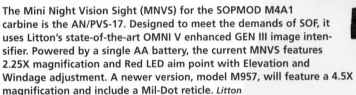

The Mini Night Vision Sight (MNVS) for the SOPMOD M4A1 carbine is the AN/PVS-17. Designed to meet the demands of SOF, it uses Litton's state-of-the-art OMNI V enhanced GEN III image intensifier. Powered by a single AA battery, the current MNVS features 2.25X magnification and Red LED aim point with Elevation and Windage adjustment. A newer version, model M957, will feature a 4.5X magnification and include a Mil-Dot reticle. *Litton*

Forward Handgrip

The Forward or Vertical Handgrip attaches to the bottom of the RIS and provides added support, giving the operator a more stable firing platform. It can be used as a monopod in a supported position and allows the operator to hold the weapon despite its overheating. The Forward Handgrip can be used to push against the assault sling and stabilize the weapon with isometric tension during CQB/CRE. Using the handgrip brings the shooter's elbows in closer or tighter to his body, consequently keeping the weapon in front of the operator. It offers quicker handling when the additional components have been attached to the weapon, thus providing more precise target acquisition.

Having numerous modifications available tends to make the soldier want to use all of them. It is not uncommon to see an operator with as many of the SOPMOD accessories on the M4A1 as he can fit. One SF MSG commented on the use of the vertical grip, "The Delta guys end up putting all the mods on the rifle, [so] that they *have* to use the vertical grip 'cause there just isn't anywhere else to hold it!" One of the problems that arose was that, with all the weight on the front-end, combined with pulling down on the vertical grip, barrels have actually bent in some instances. This bending, however slight, was just enough to cause the bullet to strike and burst the barrel, thus blowing out the hand guard. Heavier, free-floating barrels and various rail systems, hand guards and grips are being evaluated to alleviate this problem in the future. One of the drawbacks of the vertical grip is possibility of its catching on a ledge or edge of the helicopter during entry or extraction. This issue is being addressed by the evaluation of a quick release lever on the forward grip.

Quick Attach Suppressor

The Quick Attach/Detach Sound Suppressor Kit Mk4 MOD0 (QAD Suppressor) can quickly be emplaced or removed from the M4A1 carbine. With the suppressor in place, the report of the weapon is reduced by a minimum of 28 decibels (dB). As the 5.56mm round is supersonic, you will hear the bang, but it is more like a .22 caliber pistol than a 5.56mm round. With the suppressor attached, it buys some time, while the bad guys are trying to figure out, "What was that? Where did it come from?" By the time they figure out what's going on, the assault team should be in control of the situation. The suppressor will also keep the muzzle blast to a minimum, assisting the entry team in situation awareness. While the suppressor does not completely eliminate the sound, it does reduce the firing signature, that is, the flash and muzzle blasts. Using the suppressor is effective as a deceptive measure interfering with the enemy's ability to locate the shooter and take immediate action. Additionally, it reduces the need for hearing protection during CQB/CRE engagements, thus improving interteam voice communication.

The Quick Attach/Detach Sound Suppressor Kit Mk4 MOD0 (QAD Suppressor) can quickly be emplaced or removed from the M4A1 carbine. With the suppressor in place, the weapon's report is reduced by a minimum of 28 decibels (dB). The suppressor also substantially reduces muzzle flash and blast.

M203 Grenade Launcher

The Quick Attach/Detach M203 Mount and Leaf Sight, when combined with the standard M203 Grenade Launcher, provides additional firepower to the operator, giving him both a point and area engagement capability. The most commonly used ammunition is the M406 40mm projectile. Including High Explosive Dual Purpose (HEDP), this grenade has a deadly radius of 5 meters, and it used for anti-personnel and anti-light armor. Additional projectiles include: M381 HE, M386 HE, M397 Airburst, M397A1 Airburst, M433 High-explosive dual purpose (HEDP), M441 HE, M576 Buckshot, M583A1 40mm WS PARA ILLUM, M585 White star cluster, M651 CS, M661 Green star cluster, M662 Red star cluster, M676 Yellow smoke canopy, M680 White smoke canopy, M682 Red smoke canopy, M713 Ground marker—Red, M715 Ground marker—Green, M716 Ground marker—Yellow, M781 Practice, M918 Target Practice, M992 Infrared Illuminant Cartridge (IRIC), 40mm Non-lethal round, 40mm Canister round, 40mm Sponge Grenade.

This grenade has a deadly radius of five meters. The M433 multi-purpose grenade, in addition to the fragmentation effects, is capable of penetrating steel armor plate up to two inches thick. Future development in 40mm grenades will introduce airburst capability that will provide increased lethality and bursting radius through pre-fragmented, programmable high-explosive (HE) warheads.

The quick attach M203 combines flexibility and lethality into the individual weapon. Employing multiple M203 setups allows concentrated fire by bursting munitions, which are extremely useful in raids and ambushes and have the ability to illuminate or obscure the target while simultaneously delivering continuous HEDP fire. The M203 Grenade Leaf Sight attaches to the Rail Interface System for fire control.

The receiver of the M203 is manufactured from high-strength forged aluminum alloy. This provides extreme ruggedness while keeping weight to a minimum. A complete self-cocking firing mechanism, including striker, trigger, and positive safety lever, is included in the receiver. This will allow the M203 to be operated as an independent weapon, even though it's attached to the M16A1 or M16A2 rifles and the M4A1 carbine. The barrel is also made of high-strength aluminum alloy, which has been shortened from 12 to 9 inches, allowing improved balance and handling. It slides forward in the receiver to accept a round of ammunition, and then slides backward to automatically lock in the closed position, ready to fire.

Carrying out their missions in small teams, Delta operators depend on rapid deployment, mobility, and increased firepower. Where the emphasis is focused on "get in and get out" fast, the addition of the M203 brings added firepower to the already proven and outstanding M4A1 carbine.

(above) The M203 grenade launcher is a lightweight, single-shot breach-loaded 40mm weapon specifically designed for placement beneath the barrel of the M4A1 carbine. With a quick release mechanism, the addition of the M203 to M4A1 carbine creates the versatility of a weapon system capable of firing both 5.56mm ammunition as well as an expansive range of 40mm high explosive and special purpose munitions.

(left) The most commonly used ammunition is the M406 40mm projectile, which includes High Explosive Dual Purpose (HEDP); this grenade has a deadly radius of 5 meters, and is used as anti-personnel and anti-light armor.

(below) A pistol-grip arrangement for the M203, manufactured by Knight Armament Company. This attachment allows the M203 to be used as a stand-alone 40mm grenade launcher. *Knight*

Backup Iron Sight (BIS)

The Backup Iron Sight (BIS) supplies aiming ability to 300 meters, similar to the standard iron sight on the carbine. The BIS folds out of the way and allows the Day Optical Scope or Reflex Sight and night vision device to be mounted on the M4A1 carbine. In the event the optical scopes are damaged or otherwise rendered inoperable, they can be removed and the BIS will then be used to complete the mission. The sight can also be used to bore sight or confirm zero on the Reflex Sight or Visible Laser.

Combat Sling

The Combat Sling affords a hassle-free immediate and secure technique for carrying the M4A1 carbine, especially when equipped with assorted accessories from the kit. The Combat Sling can be used alone or with the mounting hardware to provide safe and ready cross-body carry or a patrol carry. If the operator is moving in close quarters in a close column formation or stack, the muzzle of the weapon is kept under control and does not sweep the operator or his teammates. The weapon is carried in a ready position to immediately engage hostile targets. Although Delta considers the SOPMOD kit standard issue, various commercial manufactures produce similar weapon slings which have also found their way into the kit bags of the Delta operators.

870P "Masterkey"

The "Masterkey" is a Remington Model 870 Police 12-gauge shotgun that has been modified to attach to the underside of the M4A1 carbine. This attachment is well liked for use in CQB operations. Using a special breaching round, the operator can blast the hinges off a door, aiding in dynamic entrance. It is also useful when loaded with buckshot rounds for anti-personnel engagements.

The Remington Model 870 Police 12-gauge shotgun, is modified so it can be attached to the underside of the M4A1 carbine. Referred to as the "Masterkey," it can use special breaching rounds for shooting off door hinges. It also uses normal shotgun ammunition, thus providing the operator with a formidable weapon for room clearing. *Knight Armament Company*

Aimpoint Comp-M

Athough not officially part of the SOPMOD kit, the Aimpoint Comp-M is in use for CQB activities. After extensive testing, the U.S. Army adopted the Aimpoint Comp-M as its red dot sighting system. Using both "eyes open" and "heads up" methods, the shooter is able to acquire the target with excellent speed and accuracy. The Comp-M sight superimposes a red dot on the target—this helps the shooter maintain constant focus, allowing him to adjust his weapon as necessary in the fast-paced shooting environment of CQB. The Comp-M is parallax free, which means the shooter does not have to compensate for parallax deviation. The sight may be mounted on the carrying handle or RIS of the M4A1.

The Comp-M sight superimposes a red dot on the target that registers with the brain, allowing the soldier to adjust his weapon according to requirements in the fast-paced shooting environment of CBQ. The Comp-M is parallax free, which means the shooter does not have to compensate for parallax deviation. The sight may be mounted on the carrying handle or RIS of the M4A1.

AN/PVS14 Night Vision Device

The AN/PVS-14D is the optimum night vision monocular ensemble for special applications. The monocular or pocket-scope can be hand held, put on a facemask, helmet mounted, or attached to a weapon. The new PVS-14D night vision monocular offers the latest state-of-the-art capability in a package that meets the rigorous demands of the U.S. military's SOF. The monocular configuration is important to shooters who want to operate with night vision while maintaining dark adaptation in the opposite eye. The kit's standard headmount assembly facilitates hands-free operation, when helmet wear is not required. The weapon mount allows use in a variety of applications from looking through the iron sights to coupling with a red dot or tritium sighting system such as the Aimpoint Comp M/ML, Trijicon ACOG system, or EOTech HDS. A compass is available to allow the user to view the bearing in the night-vision image.

specs

AN/PVS14
Resolution: 64 LP (min)
Photoresponse: 1500 (min)
Signal To Noise: 19:1 (min)
Magnification: 1X through 3X
Field Of View: 40 degrees
Diopter: +2-6
Weight: 13.8 ounces
Size: 4.5x2x2.5 inches
Battery: 2 AA
Battery Life: 30 hours

The AN/PVS-14D is the optimum night-vision monocular ensemble for special applications; it can be used as a pocket NVD or weapons sight. When coupled with a red dot or tritium sighting system such as the Aimpoint Comp M/ML, Trijicon ACOG system, or EOTech HDS, it provides a powerful tool for day/night operations.

specs

Comp-M
Optics: Band Pass Reflection Coating for compatibility with night-vision equipment
Eye Relief: Unlimited
Magnification: 1X
Power Source: 2x Silver Oxide or 1x Lithium Battery
Battery Life: 150–250 Hours (average)

Weight: 6-1/8 ounces with lens covers
Length: 5 inches with Lens Covers
Objective Diameter: 36mm
Dot Size: 3 inches at 100 yards (3MOA)
Switch: 10 positions: 8 Daylight and 2 Night Vision.

When the operator has both eyes open, one eye looks through the sight while the other concentrates on the target. The brain automatically merges the two images. This proven concept allows the operator a quick sight on target in both ambient and low light levels.

Holographic Diffraction Sight (HDS)

Manufactured by EOTech, the Holographic Diffraction Sight, as the name implies, displays holographic patterns that have been designed for instant target acquisition under any lighting situations, without covering or obscuring the point of aim. The holographic reticle can be seen through the sight, providing the operator with a large view of the target or zone of engagement. Unlike other optics, the HDS is passive and gives off no telltale signature. The heads-up full rectangular view of the HDS eliminates any blind spots, constricted vision, or tunnel vision normally associated with cylindrical sights. With both eyes open, the operator sights in on the target for a true two-eye operation.

The wide field of view of the HDS allows the operator to sight in on the target or target area while maintaining peripheral viewing through the sight if needed, up to 35 degrees off axis. A unique feature of the HDS is the fact that it works if the heads-up display window is obstructed by mud, snow, and the like. Even if the laminated window is shattered, the sight remains fully operational, with the point of aim/impact being maintained. Since many of Delta's missions favor the night, it can be used in conjunction with NVG/NVD. The hallmarks of the HDS are speed and ease of use, equating incredible accuracy and instant sight-on-target operation, which can be the difference between life and death in CQB operations.

Holographic Diffraction Sight
Optics: Holographic with Ruggedized Hood
Eye Relief: Unlimited
Magnification: 1X
Length: 4.0 inches
Weight: 6.4 ounces
Brightness Range: 28,000:1
Power Source: 2x Alkaline Batteries
Battery Life: 70 hours
Waterproof: one atmosphere
Pattern: 65 MOA outer ring with a 1MOA dot and 8 MOA quadrant ticks
Adjustments: Elevation and Windage at 1/2 MOA/click
Settings: 30 positions: 20 Daylight and 10 Night Vision

The heads up, rectangular full view of the HDS eliminates any blind spots, constricted vision, or tunnel vision normally associated with cylindrical sights. The HDS is passive and gives off no signature, which could be seen by opposing units using NVGs. Having 10 NV settings, the reticle will not "bloom" when viewed through night-vision equipment. When used in conjunction with the AN/PVS-14 NVD it provides the operator an outstanding view of the target area and allows immediate target acquisition even in the darkest of environments.

EOTech's HDS, uses the same technology found in the Heads Up Display (HUD) on the F-117 aircraft. As the name implies, it displays holographic patterns that have been designed for instant target acquisition under any lighting situations without covering or obscuring the point of aim. The holographic reticle can be seen through the sight, providing the operator with a large view of the target or zone of engagement. Using both eyes open, the operator sights in on the target for a true two-eye operation.

There are three words that describe the Holographic Diffraction Sight (HDS): Fast, Fast, and FAST! According to Mr. Van Donahue of EOTech, "When we show these sights to the operators, they say it is FM!" FM is defined as Frickin' Magic! He continues, "When Richard Marcinko (former commander and founder of the CT unit SEAL Team SIX), he took one look through the sight and said, 'This is going to save lives!'" The HDS is unparalleled in instant target acquisition under any light situations: a sight without equal for CQB operations.

EOTech holographic diffraction sight

The Series 500 HDS is a state-of-the-art optical sighting system, which for the first time employs the use of holographic sighting technology in the small-arm and medium-size-caliber weapons platforms. This holographic display employs the same technology used in the Heads-Up-Display, or HUD, of the F-117 Stealth Bomber and other U.S. aircraft. When used in Close Quarter Battle (CQB) environments, this innovative optic provides unparalleled speed, accurate target acquisition, uncompromised use of peripheral vision, and is passive, thus leaving no muzzle side signature.

The key attribute of the HDS is extremely fast reticle-to-target acquisition in multiple target situations, and in conditions where either the operator or the threat(s) are moving rapidly. As quickly as the eyes acquire the target, the holographic reticle can be locked on to the threat(s). When firing a weapon using the HDS, one eye maintains focus on the target while the other eye's natural instinctive reaction places the holographic reticle on the target. The result is an instant acquisition of the target for immediate and precise shot placement without covering or obscuring the point of aim. Whether engaging a target straight on, around corners or physical obstacles, or in awkward shooting positions, the HDS makes it easy for the operator to achieve rapid reticle-to-target lock-on. Pure and simple, the HDS locks onto the target as fast as your eyes do.

The reticle pattern of the HDS is parallax free, and the Heads Up display window provides an undistorted and unrestricted view of the target scent. The HDS standard reticle image is a 65 MOA (Minute Of Angle) ring with quadrant ticks and a 1 MOA aiming dot. The holographic patterns have been designed to be instantly visible in any light, instinctive to center regardless of shooting angle, and to remain in view while sweeping the engagement zone. Donahue explained, "With 30 levels of brightness, 20 for daylight and 10 for night vision, it is designed to operate in full daylight on a white target at 2 p.m. looking into the sun."

Other aiming reticles are available, and EOTech is working on a combination Dot and M-203 sighting system.

The HDS employs a true Heads-Up Display that eliminates blind spots, constricted vision, or the tunnel vision associated with tubed sights. All user controls are flush to the HDS's streamline housing with no protruding knobs, battery compartments, or mounting rings blocking vision at the target area. True two-eyes-open shooting is realized. Maximizing the operator's peripheral vision and ultimately gaining greater control of the engagement zone achieves instant threat identification. The Heads Up Display is constructed with a three-layer shatterproof laminate glass that is 1/4" thick for added durability. Additional protection is provided with a "roll bar" ruggedized hood.

In holography, all the information required to reconstruct the reticle image is recorded everywhere in the Heads-Up display window. If the window is obstructed by mud, snow, rain, etc., the HDS remains fully operational, with point of aim/impact being maintained. Even in such extreme cases where the laminated window is shattered, the HDS is fully functional! As long as the operator can see through any portion of the window, the entire reticle pattern is visible on target and the operator can still engage with confidence.

The HDS delivers an impressive 28,000:1 bright-to-low contrast ratio. Reticles can be easily seen against white targets in desert or tundra environments, then placed in super low-light conditions without "washing out" the target scene. For extreme low-light conditions, engaging the HDS's night-vision setting (Model 550 only) increases the contrast ratio to an incredible 28,000,000:1.

The HDS does not emit any muzzle-side-position-revealing light signature, therefore the projected reticle pattern is visible only to the operator. Even Gen III night-vision equipment cannot detect any muzzle side signature of the operator's position. All optical surfaces are flat and treated with anti-reflective coatings, eliminating additional muzzle side signature due to reflective glare. No need for glare-elimination filters that reduce the effective light transmission and further dim the target area.

Though the HDS is passive and gives off no signature, it can be used in tandem with the AN/PVS-14 Night Vision Device. The HDS has 10 NV settings, the reticle will not "bloom" when viewed through the NVD. This arrangement provides the operator with an outstanding view of the target area, and immediate target acquisition even in the darkest of environments.

Without a doubt, the EOTech HDS has no equal when the operator requires instant target acquisition in the CQB environment.

(below) Magazines loaded with 5.56mm 62 grain ammunition. To say Delta operators shoot a lot of ammunition is an understatement. One operator said they shot so much in a single day that, "[their] thumbs were bleeding from loading so many magazines." Delta operators take their shooting very seriously. In addition to the high-tech shooting facility at the Delta complex, there are four additional shooting houses located around Fort Bragg to which Delta operators have access.

(above) Two SF sergeants come ashore to conduct a beach reconnaissance. This view shows a wide assortment of SOPMOD accessories on their M4A1 rifles. The M4A1 is fitted with the suppressor; and Trijicon ACOG, the weapon on the right is equipped with the Aimpoint COMP-M and the AN/PEQ-2.

2001–2005 Enhanced Carbine and Subcomponents + SOPMOD Block 2

Block 2 Upgrades will address reliability, controllability, safety, accuracy, and ergonomics. A summary of the Block 2 modifications include:

Enhanced Combat Optical Sight (ECOS): a versatile, multi-function day optics with illuminated reticle for limited night-fighting capability. It is a sight that combines the capabilities of the ACOG 4x32, COMP-M, and Reflex II into one scope. Allowing CQB capabilities (0–200 meters) with 1X power coupled with long-range (100–600 meters) target recognition, acquisitions and engagement, with fixed, variable, or switchable power settings from the 4x–8x range. Other capabilities that may be incorporated in the ECOS would be ranges finding, video output, GPS, round count, temperature sensor, and so on.

Image Intensifier Module, (I^2M): night-vision optics to intensify the imaging and aiming capability of the weapon with current optics and the projected ECOS.

Digital Daylight Image Video Module (DDIVM): a miniature daylight-image-capture device for recording still and motion images, providing a real-time image of the shooter's-eye view. This will allow digital transmission to the user of future devices, for example, Heads-Up Display and external transmitters.

Thermal Image Module (TIM): will give the operator a thermal imaging and aiming capability. The TIM may include video output, range finding, GPS sensor, and flux-gate compass.

Enhance Grenade Launcher Module (EGLM), consisting of three subsystems: the launcher, Self-Ranging Ballistic Sight (SRBS), and the Low-Velocity Pre-Frag-mented Programmable High Explosive (LV-PPHE) 40mm munitions. The airburst capability will provide increased lethality and bursting radius through a prefragmented programmable high-explosive warhead. The module may be mounted beneath the barrel of the M4A1 or used with a QAD Buttstock for stand-alone operation.

Rangefinder Module (RM): a miniaturized version of the commercial rangefinders currently available. It will mount on the rail system and be compatible for integration with the other components or as a stand-alone device.

Integrated Pointer-Illuminator Module (IPIM): will combine the capabilities of the current AN/PEQ-2 IR Pointer Illuminator, AN/PEQ-5 Visible Laser, and the Visible Light Illuminator (VLI). The module will have improved IR and visible aiming and illumination.

Enhance Shotgun Module (ESM): provides a 12-gauge shotgun, which will be an enhancement to the Remington 870 "Master Key"; will be used for door breeching, antipersonnel, and less-than-lethal capabilities. It will be mounted underneath the M4A1 barrel, similar to the mounting of the M203 and be configured to be used as a stand-alone weapon.

Heat Source Detection Module (HSDM): will be capable of detecting and locating individuals hiding in foliage, buildings, etc. Visual imagery from the TIM component may be fed to the ECOS.

Improved 5.56mm ammunition will allow more flexible use of the M4A1 carbine. This will include subsonic munitions for engaging targets at close range or for sentry suppression, and an over-the-beach (OTB) round, which will allow the carbine to fire even when flooded with water. Additionally, the ammunition will have an improved armor piercing round for engaging hard targets.

Battery Recharger/Blasting Machine (BRBM): This item would have a dual purpose. First, it would be able to recharge the batteries that power many of the SOPMOD accessories, and second, the unit could double as a blasting machine to detonate Claymore mines.

Shot Counter (SC): a component that will enable the armory personnel to readily determine the number of rounds fired through the weapon and identify maintenance and replacement of the carbine's components.

Over The Beach Receiver (OTBR): a separate ongoing project that will permit the firing of the weapon under water, and also immediately upon exiting the water without the delay of draining the weapon.

Family of Muzzle Brake/Suppressors (FMBS): will reduce the weapon's flash and sound signatures. Systems include a small ergonomic CQB suppressor, a standard carbine suppressor, a high-accuracy suppressor and a machine-gun suppressors. It is the hope that one or two suppressors may accomplish all of these requirements; however, technical constraints may limit this possibility.

Laser Protection and Protection from Optical Augmentation (LPPOA): devices and methods to protect both the operator and the weapon's optics and optical systems from the threat of laser damage and laser detection.

Sustained Fire Assembly (SFA): the introduction of a receiver assembly that would allow the safe and effective firing of belt-feed ammunition and high-capacity magazines.

Chamber Bore Sight (CBS): will fit the standard 5.56mm chamber and will project a visible beam that will align with the rifle bore to allow bore sight of the weapon with both day and night sights as well as aiming lasers.

Enhanced Bayonet/Field Knife (EBFK): This combination bayonet and knife would attach to the barrel of the weapon as opposed to a bayonet lug. With the preferences of the operators for their Randalls, Gerbers, and other knives of personal choice this may not see much use in the "Force."

Other Block 2 upgrades include the introduction of a more ergonomic vertical grip. This could be mechanically adjustable or boiled like a SCUBA gear mouthpiece, as well as special-purpose receivers such as an 11.5-inch barrel for CQB.

2005–2010 Integrated Carbine (IC) + SOPMOD Block 3

The current SOPMOD kit makes use of various accessories, which can be bulky, heavy, and prone to snagging during movement. The IC modification concentrates on integrating these various components into a well balanced, ergonomic, and highly reliable weapon.

The SOPMOD Block 3 upgrade will see a more streamlined version of the M4A1 carbine, designated the Integrated Carbine (IC). The IC design will incorporate all of the aspects of the M4A1 carbine, getting the optics and lasers *off* the weapon and *into* the weapon itself, as well as the complement of a thermal sighting device. There will be an addition of mode switches—buttons to the vertical grip to activate lasers, thermal, visible, and so on. The thermal sighting component may very well have the operational capability to be linked to JSTARS.

Modifications that may be incorporated into the IC are: visible laser component for pointing and aiming,

which would operate on a pulsed beam and patter and a visible light; near IR laser for aiming and pointing; a range-finding component with information sent to a display or onto the weapon reticle; automatic ranging and ballistic solutions; upgrading the ECOS with ranging information, weapon cant, barrel temperature, and a shot count. All items would be readily mountable and easily removable at the operator's discretion.

Through the various iterations, modifications, and upgrades the M4A1 and SOPMOD will go through over the next decade, the M4A1 carbine will most assuredly be a state-of-the-art weapon system for twenty-first-century missions. The Delta operators will have more than the necessary firepower and optical capability to engage any terrorist threat or other mission parameters that they may encounter.

> Currently under consideration for possible addition to the SOPMOD kit is the Lightweight Shotgun System, (LSS). Attachment is similar to the M-203 40mm grenade launcher: the LSS mounts under the barrel of the M4A1 carbine. The LSS is a 12-gauge weapon that would most likely be carried by the point man, giving him an extra punch. It would also prove useful in the Military Operations Urban Terrain (MOUT) operations and in CQB missions. *USASOC*

HK Submachine Guns and Pistols

Although Delta has moved to the M4A1 as its primary weapon, the HK MP5 series of submachine guns can still be found in the inventory of this ultra-elite unit. The MP5 offers a hard-hitting, compact, and reliable weapon that has its place in certain missions.

MP5

There was a time when you could not spell CQB without an H&K. Manufactured by Heckler & Koch, Germany, the MP5 series has become the hallmark of CT operators worldwide, and Delta is no exception. While the "Force" *has* moved to the M4A1 carbine as its primary weapon, there are those who believe the MP5 still has a viable place in CT and CQB operations.

Heckler & Koch offers more than 120 variants of the MP5 submachine gun to deal with any tactical situation an operator may encounter. Depending on the model of HK weapon, modes of fire are SAFE, semi-automatic, two-round burst, three-round burst, and sustained (firing automatic as long as the trigger is held back). All MP5 versions have identical subassemblies, ensuring that many of the components of the various weapons are interchangeable within the HK weapon system this gives the MP5 series of submachine guns exceptional flexibility to facilitate almost any mission parameter. *Defense Visual Information Center*

The MP5 series of weapons are compact, durable, hard-hitting—and all right, just plain sexy—and they remain a favorite of some shooters. For the times when you don't want a cartridge capable of penetrating 3/4 inch of steel plate (that is, 5.56mm), and when you want something more compact, more concealable, and more maneuverable, the MP5 series of sub-guns still remains a practical option. An MP5 makes sense in certain scenarios: extremely close quarters or thin walls—but even then, you would probably want a few guys on the team with more firepower, for example, the M4A1. The choice of weapons will largely remain mission dependent, and thus you will still find the MP5s in Delta's armory. You will also find these submachine guns in the inventories of other operators schooled in the art of CT/CQB, for example, the U.S. Navy SEALs, FBI-HRT, and the British SAS.

The submachine guns in the MP5 family of submachine guns are automatic weapons, simple to handle as well as fast and accurate, whether firing from the shoulder or the hip. The MP5 employs the same delayed blowback-operated roller-locked bolt system found in the proven HK G3 automatic rifle. All the characteristics

of HK—reliability, ease of handling, simple maintenance, and safety—are accentuated on the MP5. Firing from the closed-bolt position during all modes of fire makes MP5 submachine guns extremely accurate and controllable. The weapon's high accuracy results from the fixed barrel, which is cold forged together with the cartridge chamber. The recoil of the MP5 is extremely smooth, allowing the shooter to obtain highly accurate shot placement. It fires a 9mm Parabellum pistol round, usually carried in a 30-round magazine, and it is often equipped with a dual magazine holder. An operator with an MP5 can be very effective when encountering a terrorist in a hostage situation or when engaging other mission-critical targets.

Common throughout each of the MP5 series of weapons is the capability to use various interchangeable assemblies and components. This provides the ability for operators to train with one weapon group while giving them competence with the entire weapon system. The series also includes an accessory claw-lock scope mount and telescopic sight. HK scope mounts as wells as other mounts, such as ARMS mounts, attach to the weapons without any special tools at special points that ensure 100 percent return to zero.

MP5-N

The MP5-N was developed by HK especially for the U.S. Navy SEALs. The MP5 "Navy" model comes standard with an ambidextrous trigger group and threaded barrel. The MP5-N fires from a closed and locked bolt in either the semiautomatic or automatic modes. This sub/gun is recoil operated and has a unique delayed roller locked-bolt system, a retractable butt stock, a removable suppressor, and illuminating flashlight integral to the forward hand guard. The flashlight is operated by a pressure switch custom fitted to the pistol grip. The basic configuration of this weapon makes for an ideal size, weight, and capable close quarters battle weapon system.

The MP5-N comes standard with an ambidextrous trigger group and threaded barrel. The MP5-N fires from a closed and locked bolt in either the semiautomatic or automatic modes. This sub-gun is recoil operated and has a unique delayed-roller locked-bolt system, retractable buttstock, removable suppressor, and illuminating flashlight integral to the forward hand guard. The flashlight is operated by a pressure switch custom fitted to the pistol grip. *Defense Visual Information Center*

MP5K

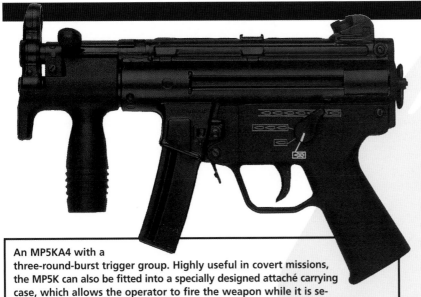

The MP5K is a compact version of the M5P, referred to as a *Maschinenpistole*. The "K" designation is German for *kurz*, or "short." The MP5K is the ultimate covert close-quarters weapon. Weighing in at only 4.4 pounds, and less than 13 inches in length, the MP5K is easily concealed and carried. All MP5Ks can be fitted with an optional folding buttstock. You'll often find the sub/gun carried in a special shoulder harness for instant access. The MP5K can also be fired from inside a specially designed briefcase.

An MP5KA4 with a three-round-burst trigger group. Highly useful in covert missions, the MP5K can also be fitted into a specially designed attaché carrying case, which allows the operator to fire the weapon while it is secured to the inside of the case. It is shown here with a compact 15-round 9mm magazine, which is interchangeable with the 30-round magazines of the MP5 series. *Heckler & Koch*

MP5K-PDW

The MP5K-PDW (Personal Defense Weapon) is a compact submachine gun that was intended for use by vehicle operators, aircrew members, security details, and other SOF that have need of a small but powerful weapon. While similar in operation to the full-size MP5s, the MP5K-PDW's size and weight make this weapon the ideal choice in situations in which an M4A1 or full-sized MP5 would be unmanageable, and a handgun would have insufficient fire power. Equipped with a folding buttstock and threaded barrel, the MP5K-PDW is an extremely adaptable weapon.

The PDW or Personal Defense Weapon is a new HK offering in 9mm. Compact and hard hitting, it would serve well for bodyguards and other occasions when a larger weapon would be cumbersome or impractical. With the stock and forward grip extended, it provides a steady firing position for the user. *Heckler & Koch*

MP5SD

For missions whose paramount requirements are stealth and secrecy, requiring fully integrated sound and flash suppression, the operators may turn to the HK MP5SD models. The model type, SD, comes from the German term for "sound dampened" or *Schalldampfer*. The removable sound suppressor is integrated into the MP5's design and measures up to the normal length and profile of a standard unsuppressed submachine gun. The MP5SD uses an integral aluminum or optional wet-technology stainless steel sound suppressor. It does not require use of subsonic ammunition for effective sound reduction, as do most conventional sound-suppressed submachine guns. The MP5SD3 has an S-E-F trigger group and the MP5SD6 has a three-round burst group.

Model	MP5A3	MP5-N	MP5K	MP5K-PDW	MP5SD3/SD6
Caliber	9mm Parabellum (9x19 NATO)				
Weight	6.47 lbs	6.47 lbs	4.40 lbs	6.14 lbs	7.63 lbs
Barrel length	8.85 in	8.85 in	4.50 in	5.50 in	5.73 in
Overall Length					
Stock Extended	27.25 in	27.25 in	12.80 in	23.75 in	31.69 in
Stock Retracted	21.00 in	21.00 in	12.80 in	14.50 in	25.68 in
Cyclic Rate	800 rpm	800 rpm	–	–	800 rpm
Suppressor Length	–	–	–	–	12 in

The MP5SD has a built-in integral sound suppressor or sound-damping device. The model type, SD, comes from the German term for "Sound Dampened" or *Schalldampfer*. The MP5SD3 has the Navy trigger group, Safe, Semi, Burst, and Full-Auto. The MP5SD has been the weapon of choice among counter-terrorist groups for a number of years. The SD3 has a retractable stock, while the SD4 designates the fixed-stock version.

Some say that S-E-F on the MP5 series trigger group stands for *safe, easy,* and *fun*! While this may be the case in practice, the official HK nomenclature for the sub-gun is as follows: S-E-F are the first letters for the German words for Safe (*Sicher*), Single Fire/Semi (*Einzelfeuer*), and Burst/Full Auto (*Feuerstoss*). Other versions of the fire selector will feature a pictograph showing single bullet in white for Safe, single bullet in red for semi-automatic, three bullets in red for three-round burst, and seven bullets in red for full automatic.

G36

Just as the Delta operators have reassessed the 9mm for CT/CQB missions, so has HK. Heckler & Koch have introduced the G36, a modular weapon system in caliber 5.56mm. Compared to the Colt weapons, HK representatives say, "The M4 is a Ford; the G36 is a Chevy." Both are quality weapon systems; the G36 just gives the operators another option. Manufactured almost completely of carbon fiber-reinforced polymer material and using a simple, self-regulating gas system, the G36 provides the operator with a lightweight weapon capable of delivering high performance but requiring low maintenance. Being a modular system, the barrel of the G36 can be exchanged by the unit's armorers to construct a rifle, carbine, or light support variant using the same common receiver. The G36 is also available in a compact version. The G36 compact carbine features a 9-inch barrel and is actually shorter than an MP5 with the buttstock folded. Features include an accessory vertical grip, optional Aimpoint reflex sight, shortened forearm with six hard points for attaching accessories, and shortened four-prong flash hider.

G36 features include 30-round translucent polymer magazines, which lock together without magazine clamps. A 100-round dual drum magazine is also available. An ambidextrous safety/selector lever allows for easy actuation without adjusting the firing grip. An ambidextrous cocking lever doubles as forward assist and can be used to silently chamber a round. A variety of trigger group mechanisms are available for the G36, including the standard "SEF" group, "Navy" trigger group with safe, semi-automatic, and fully automatic modes of fire and pictogram markings, as well as a single-fire trigger group that prevents fully automatic fire. The weapon has a chrome-plated, cold hammer forged barrel with 1 in 7 inch twist rifling. An integral mounting rail allows the HK UTL (Universal Tactical Light) to be installed in seconds. Downward ejection of spent cartridge cases reduces visual signature.

Model	UMP45	UMP40	G36	G36 Compact	G36K	MG36
Caliber	.45 ACP	.40 S&W	5.56mm	5.56mm	5.56mm	.56mm
Weight	4.93 lbs	4.63 lbs	7.28 lbs	6.28 lbs	6.62 lbs	7.87 lbs
Barrel length	7.87 in	7.87 in	18.90 in	8.98 in	12.52 in	18.90 in
Overall Length						
Stock in/out	17.72/ 27.17 in	17.72/ 27.17 in	29.84/ 39.29 in	19.69/ 28.27 in	24.21/ 33.78 in	29.84/ 39.29 in

The G36 Commando short carbine. Chambered for 5.56mm ammunition, this carbine is actually shorter than the MP5. The G36 Commando possesses six hard points for mounting various accessories. It is seen here with the Aimpoint Comp-M/ML and the forward vertical foregrip. With the advent of terrorists now wearing body armor, the concern of under-penetration of the 9mm has warranted CT units to move to 5.56mm ammunition. The G36 carbine gives the operators one more tool to choose from in their life-and-death missions. *Heckler & Koch*

UMP

The UMP is a new offering from HK. This state-of-the-art submachine gun is chambered for .45 caliber ammunition, offering operators the advantages of light weight, reliability, and precision accuracy with low-felt recoil. Like all HK submachine guns, the UMP fires from the closed-bolt position. The UMP45 is equipped with a 25-round magazine with an accurate range of 100 yards and beyond. The UMP folding buttstock reduces the overall length of the weapon by nearly 10 inches when closed. The UMP45 is capable of firing a wide assortment of .45 ACP ammunition—including subsonic and supersonic loads, cartridges assembled with ball, high-performance hollow-point, and enhanced velocity +P ammunition.

Hard points molded into the polymer receiver of the weapon allow for the attachment of a wide assortment of optional mounting rails and accessories, such as assault sights, tactical lights, lasers, and vertical fore grips. UMP firing mode choices include semiautomatic only, semiautomatic and two-round burst, or semiautomatic and fully automatic modes of fire.

UMP submachine gun, built for the hard-hitting .45ACP cartridge. With various hard points and the addition of a Picatinny rail, various scopes, lights, and laser-aiming devices can be mounted. This UMP has been fitted with Aimpoint Comp-M/ML red dot forward vertical grip and a Quick Connect sound suppressor. The fire selector shows a pictogram of safe, semi-automatic, and full automatic. A 25-round magazine feeds it. *Heckler & Koch*

PSG1

The PSG1 is HK's offering for sniper operations. It's been heralded as the world's most accurate semi-automatic sniper rifle: a 7.62mm precision marksman rifle featuring a free-floating polygonal heavyweight barrel, and a trigger mechanism with a three-pound trigger pull. The barrel and receiver assembly are virtually locked together tightly enough so that—just like the operating parts in a glass-bedded bolt-action rifle—there is minimal movement or play. This allows the roller-locked action of the PSG1 to return and lock up consistently shot after shot after shot, making it one of the most accurate semi-automatic sniper rifles available.

PSG1 features include: adjustable buttstock, pivoting butt plate, adjustable check piece, fixed mount for zero retention, adjustable Swiss-made tripod, 5-round or 20-round magazine capacity, trigger shoe, and adjustable contoured handgrip.

specs

PSG1
Caliber: 7.62mm NATO
Photoresponse: 1500 (min)
Weight: (without magazine and optics) 17.86 pounds
Barrel Length: 25.59 inches
Length: 47.565 inches

MK 23 MOD 0 - SOCOM Pistol

Another member of the H&K family is the MK 23 MOD 0, SOCOM pistol. There is a tradeoff for knockdown power and accuracy, that is, more weight or size. Some argue that the MK 23 is too large and ungainly for real-world ops; we will let operators make that call. The HK MK23 pistol has an effective recoil-reduction system, which reduces recoil forces to the components and shooter by 40 percent. It is a double/single action pistol with a 12-round capacity magazine.

A high-temperature rubber O-ring on the barrel—an innovative design feature—seals the barrel in the slide until unlocking. To meet operational environmental requirements, the pistol was tested at +160 and -60 degrees F, exposed to two hours of seawater at 66 feet, used in surf, sand, mud, with icing, and unlubricated. A special maritime surface coating protected the pistol from any corrosion in all of these environments.

The barrel is threaded to accept attachments such at the KAC sound suppressor and the frame is grooved to accept the ITI Laser Aiming Module (LAM). The weapon is aimed by three-dot white light of self-lumi-nous tritium dots, or the LAM. Another unique feature of the MK23 is the decocking lever. This allows the hammer to be lowered quietly, which can prove to be quite beneficial on a covert operation when "bad guys" are around.

When the hammer is down the safety lever is blocked in the fire position so that the pistol is always ready for double-action operation. When the hammer is cocked and the safety set to "safe," the decocker is blocked so that the pistol is ready for single-action operation by moving the safety to the "fire" position. The extended slide relapse and ambidextrous magazine release are easily actuated without adjustment of the firing grip.

An MK23 MOD 0 SOCOM pistol. Designed specifically for U.S. SOF, it is chambered for .45 caliber ACP ammunition. Although an exceptionally accurate handgun, some operators feel the weapon to be too large for normal operation parameters. With its entry into service in 1996, it was the first .45 caliber pistol to be employed in U.S. military service since the introduction of the Government Model 1911.

Laser Aiming Module (LAM)

The LAM is the result of over four years of development by Insight Technology, USSOCOM, and the Naval Surface Warfare Center, Crane Division. The LAM contains visible and infrared lasers for aiming, an infrared illuminator, and a visible white light.

The current model LAM is designed to be securely attached to the MK23 by using the mounting grooves on the frame of the weapon. Attachment of the LAM does not affect the functionality of the weapon, and the unit can be detached and reattached to the pistol while maintaining a repeatable bore-sight of better than .4 inches at 25 meters.

The LAM can operate in one of four selected operational modes. This is accomplished by rotating the selector switch of the side of the LAM to the desired position. The four modes of operation are: Visible Laser Only, Visible Laser/Flashlight, Infrared Laser Only, and Infrared Laser/Illuminator. Once the mode has been selected, the

LAM is easily activated in either a momentary or steady-on condition by depressing a switch lever located just forward of the pistol's trigger guard. Internal bore-sight adjusters allow the LAM to be precisely zero to the weapon.

The current-issue sound suppressor deployed by USSOCOM for the HK MK23 pistol is the .45 Cal Suppressor manufactured by Knight Armament Company. One of the unique features of this suppressor is that the operator may loosen and index to 10 different positions. This allows the operator to adjust the weapon's point of impact within two inches. Constructed of stainless steel, the suppressor is welded to five (star-shaped sections) baffles. Weighing in at one pound, the KAC suppresser can be attached to or removed from the MK23 in a matter of seconds. It requires very low maintenance and has an extremely long life. Decibels reduction is rated at 38db (wet) or 28db (dry). SOF operators report that with the suppressor on all you hear is the sound of the action.

USP and USP Tactical

Based on the Mark 23 Model 0, the HK USP (Universal Self-loading Pistol) and USP Tactical are smaller. Both pistols are configured for .45-caliber ammunition, with the USP also available in a 9mm and .40 caliber. The USP features an ambidextrous magazine release just behind the trigger guard. This allows operation using the thumb or index finger without adjusting the grip on the weapon. The pistols have grooves on the lower side to facilitate the mounting of lights and laseraiming devices.

The USP Tactical has a threaded O-ring barrel that will allow the use of the KAC suppressor manufactured for the MK23. The rear target sight has adjustments for windage and elevation and features a three-dot tritium sight. The extractor of the pistol doubles as a loaded chamber indicator; however, as operators are taught, the only sure way to be 100 percent sure of a loaded chamber is to move the slide back slightly and look. Unlike the Mark 23, the USP Tactical does not feature a separate decocking lever.

The USP 45 Tactical is an enhanced version of the USP45. The Tactical version gives operators many of the features of the MK23, but in a smaller package. It features an extended-thread barrel with an O-ring to allow the attachment of the Knight Armament Company's sound suppressor. The USP Tactical uses a 12-round magazine, just like the MK23. *Heckler & Koch*

Model	USP	USP	USP	USP Tactical	MK23 MOD 0
Caliber:	45 ACP	9mm	.40 S&W	45 ACP	45 ACP
Weight:					
(w/o Magazine):	1.74 lbs	1.65 lbs	1.66 lbs	1.90 lbs	4.22 lbs (with suppressor)
Length:	7.87 in	7.64 in	7.64 in	8.64 in	9.65 in (16.56 w/suppressor)
Barrel Length:	5.875 in	4.25 in	4.25 in	5.09 in	5.875 in
Capacity:	12 + 1 staggered	15+1	13+1	12+1	12+1

(left) The Universal Self-loading Pistol, or USP, comes in 9mm, .40 caliber S&W and, as seen here, the .45 caliber ACP. The USP was based on the Mark 23 platform and uses a modified Browning type action. The recoil-reduction system features a spring within a spring, which without doubt dampens the felt recoil of this hard-hitting semi-automatic pistol.

(bottom) The HK21E General Purpose Machine Gun with a cyclic rate of 800 rpm. This MG provides semi-automatic rifle precision in a belt-fed 7.62mm weapon. This weapon was often placed into service as an alternate to the aging M60 machine gun. With the adoption of the M240B by the U.S. Army, the MH21 may start seeing more shelf time.

The Armory

While the Colt M4A1 and the HK MP5s are the "bread and butter" weapons in use with Delta, the Delta armory is filled with an extensive assortment of other weaponry. The Armory includes everything from pistols to shotguns, sniper rifles to anti-tank weapons; all of U.S., foreign, and enemy origins. Delta's armorers maintain these weapons and provide a vast selection to meet any mission profile to which the operators may find themselves assigned.

The M136 AT4 is a lightweight, self-contained, man-portable anti-armor weapon. Inside the expendable one-piece fiberglass-wrapped tube is a free flight, fin-stabilized, rocket-type cartridge. The launcher is watertight for ease of transportation and storage.

(left) Delta operators are masters of their craft, whether using the latest weaponry from the armory or older weapons. Their missions often send them into third-world environments where they may come across anti-quated firearms. This assortment of pistols includes (beginning at the up-per left) Scorpion, Glock, Browning Hi-Power, Russian Pistolet Makarov, and HK USP.

(lower left) The .45 ACP remains the weapon of choice for the consummate Delta operator. One of the custom .45s in use with Delta is the Wilson Combat CQB. Accurate to 1 inch at 25 yards, this semi-automatic pistol fea-tures a two-tone finish of matte black with an Armor-Tuff corrosion-resist-ant finish in olive drab. Magazine ca-pacity is eight rounds, and it has a tactical combat sight with tritium in-serts for aiming in low light levels.

Pistols

The main use for the pistol is as a secondary or backup weapon. At times when the mission dictates, it may be employed for delicate or light and fast operations, hostage snatch, or hostage-situation takedown. Volumes have been written on the capability differ-ences between 9mm and .45 caliber munitions and handguns. We will not add to this debate here. In fact, while Delta Force has an assortment of pistols from which to choose, including the 9mm parabellum, it has never adopted the 9mm and opted instead to stay with the tried-and-true hard-hitting .45-caliber weapons. Suffice it to say that when it comes to handguns, spe-cial operation operators always come back to their first love, the .45 caliber, established as the best choice for CQB because of its huge knockdown power. For this reason, you will see a wide assortment of .45 semi-au-tomatics among the operators. Among the favorites are the Colt National Match, Wilson Combat, and Les Baer.

These custom-built handguns are fine-tuned to the op-erators' personal preferences, so it becomes an extension of the individual.

If the mission calls for lightweight equipment, then the Sig Sauer, CZ-75 or M9 Beretta are among the pre-ferred. This also provides the operator with twice as many rounds as the .45s—usually 15, versus 8. During missions, an operator will tend to carry the pistol either on a drop-down holster attached to his leg, or attached to an assault vest. Carrying the pistol on the leg allows quick access, but it can flop around and sometimes catch on ledges or edges. Wearing the pistol on the vest reverses these concerns, but then it can become tougher to access. For times when operators will be running covertly, performing a site recon, or other non-descript mission, they will employ a vast array of shoul-der, belt, and ankle holsters to accommodate their weapon(s) of choice.

Pistols (continued)

When it comes to shooting proficiency, the operators of Delta Force are without equal. They are trained and practiced in the fine art of shooting, whether standing, sitting, kneeling, crouching, or prone. Whether they are in a vehicle, a helicopter, a zodiac, or moving on foot, they are capable of engaging and neutralizing any target that may present itself. Operators practice these skills relentlessly to maintain their high level of expertise. Thousands of rounds will be expended to assure that, when it matters, the Delta shooters will be on the mark. It is not unusual to see more than a few bleeding thumbs on the firing line due to operators loading magazine upon magazine of ammunition as they practice their lethal trade.

The characteristic posture during CQB is based on the isosceles stance, allowing the torso to rotate from side to side, much like a turret. This positioning allows the shooter to quickly respond to any enemy threat regardless of the direction. The Delta operator is an expert combat marksman schooled in the fundamentals of shooting: stance, grip, sight alignment, sight picture, breath control, trigger control, follow-through, and recovery. If you understand and acclimate yourself to those eight points, you will get hits—whether you are standing on the corner, sitting in a HUMMV, or jogging down the street, you will hit your target.

The M9 was introduced as the standard-issue sidearm for U.S. troops in 1985. Although it was never adopted by Delta, there are occasions when a 9mm has its place. Seen here is an M9 Beretta with a Knight Armament Company sound suppressor. The smooth cylindrical suppressor is manufactured of anodized aluminum with a steel attachment system. Weighing a mere 6 ounces, it can be attached or removed in 3 seconds.

Shotguns

When you think of the weapons in use by Delta and other CT organizations around the world, images of submachine guns, assault rifles, and custom pistols come to mind. Although less often thought of, the combat shotgun has a key role in CT and DA missions alike and is a welcome addition to the team's weapon selection. The shotgun has been used in combat from the trenches of World War I to the close-in jungle fighting of the Pacific during World War II. Whether the shotgun was a pump action or semi-automatic, it proved highly effective in laying out a devastating blast with an assortment of shot. During the Vietnam War it was common practice among some special op units to arm the point man with a 12-gauge shotgun.

A wide range of shotguns can be found in the hands of the operators: the Remington 870, Mossberg 500 series, Franchi SPAS12, and the Benelli series, to name a few. With the trend of warfare leaning more toward the urban environment, it is becoming Standard Operation Procedure (SOP) to include a shotgun among the team—not only full-size shotguns, but also specialized modifications such as the aforementioned 870P "Masterkey" or the SOCOM Light Shotgun System. Useful in CQB, the shotgun can be used for manual breaching or anti-personnel actions.

A shortened version of the Remington M-870 is seen here—slung ready for ballistic breaching. Using a shotgun with a variety of ammunition, such as #9 birdshot, "shock locks," and other specialty ammo will defeat a door, primarily the locking mechanism.

Often the weapon of choice for the entry team is the 12-gauge Remington M-870 shotgun, seen here with pistol grip. From breaching locked doors to laying down a wall of lead shot, the shotgun is a versatile tool for CQB operations. *Defense Visual Information Center*

The Mossberg 590 nine-shot with ghost ring sights uses a synthetic stock with rubber recoil pad. This shotgun is a 12-gauge model with a 20-inch barrel. *Mossberg*

The Mossberg 590 nine-shot with standard front bead sight. The upper is equipped with a heat shield and special shell holder in the stock capable of holding four additional shotgun shells. *Mossberg*

Mossberg 500 six-shot with ghost ring sights, 18.5-inch barrel with a cylinder bore choke. The Mossberg 12-gauge shotgun may also be modified with a pistol grip, making it a good choice for a breaching weapon. *Mossberg*

The M1 Entry model comes equipped with a 14-inch cylinder bore barrel. Benelli M1 features chrome-lined barrels, corrosion-resistant finishes, and high-strength synthetic buttstocks. A selection of sights, barrel options, and buttstock choices permit the M1 shotgun to be modified for special missions. *Benelli*

The M1 Tactical is one of the numerous 12-gauge shotguns from Benelli. It includes special features such as a speed loader, recoil reducer, adjustable ghost ring sights, and optic rail. The M1 Tactical is available with a 26-inch barrel and an extended magazine tube. The M1 can fire five rounds in less than one second. *Benelli*

The M3 is a combination pump/semi-automatic shotgun. It blends the unique features of the semi-automatic Benelli M1 shotgun with the added flexibility of a manual pump action. The M3–Super 90s type of action can easily be selected during field use, by simply rotating a selector ring attached to the forearm to choose the preferred firing mode. The semi-automatic mode on the M3 handles all standard 12-gauge shotgun shells. The pump mode not only handles standard shells, but gas grenades, flares, and non-lethal ammunition as well. *Benelli*

The M4–Super 90 is the newest 12-gauge shotgun from Benelli. The operator has the choice of three modular buttstocks and two barrels. These modifications can rapidly be re-configured without tools. Also adaptable are the operating controls and sling attachment points, which have been optimized for left- and right-handed users. Sights are the ghost-ring style, adjustable for windage and elevation in the field, using a cartridge rim. The addition of a Picatinny rail allows mounting of both conventional and night-vision sights, while retaining metallic-sight capability. *Benelli*

(left) When the operation calls for the hard-hitting 5.56mm ammunition of the M4A1 and the compactness of the HK MP5, the Force may utilize the Colt Commando assault rifle. Its shortened barrel aids in concealment for stealth movements and covert operations, yet still provides the operator with a formidable round. *Defense Visual Information Center*

(right) The M14 rifle was the standard service rifle until it was replaced in the late 1960s by the M16A1 rifle. Although it has been replaced, the M14 has found a home among several U.S. SOF operators. Delta Force continues to maintain this rifle in its inventory, as do the U.S. Navy SEALs. During Task Force Ranger in Somalia, Delta sniper SFC Randall D. Shughart choose to carry the M14 over the M4 or MP5, due to the solid takedown capabilities of the 7.62mm round.

M249 Squad Automatic Weapon

The SAW is an air-cooled, belt-fed, gas-operated automatic weapon that fires from the open-bolt position. It has a regulator for selecting either normal (750 rounds per minute [rpm]) or maximum (1,000 rpm) rate of fire. The SAW, or 5.56mm M249, is an individually portable, gas-operated, magazine-fed or disintegrating metallic linked-belt-fed, light machine gun with fixed headspace and quick-change barrel feature. The M249 engages point targets out to 800 meters, firing the improved NATO standard 5.56mm cartridge. The SAW forms the basis of firepower for the fire team. The gunner has the option of using 30-round M16 magazines or linked ammunition from pre-loaded 200-round plastic magazines. The gunner's basic load is 600 rounds of linked ammunition.

The SAW can utilize standard 20- and 30-round M4/M16 magazines, which are inserted in a magazine well in its bottom. Utilizing the same 5.56mm ammunition as the M4, it allows the teams to carry common ammunition loads. The M249 is capable of engaging targets out to 800 meters. Here the modified SAW is seen with a collapsible stock. This soldier is wearing Bolle T800R Tactical Goggles.

(below left) The AK-47 and AKM 51x39mm assault rifle is the preferred weapon of many terrorists and one of the most proliferated weapons in the world. Delta operators not only know how to deal with them as a threat, but also how to operate and employ them should the need arise. Having their roots in Special Forces, these warriors are familiar with a variety of weapons—U.S. and foreign, friend and foe, old and new.

(below right) The M249 Squad Automatic Weapon (SAW) is an individually portable, air-cooled, belt-fed, gas-operated light machine gun that fires from the open-bolt position. The standard ammunition load is 200 rounds of 5.56mm ammunition in disintegrating belts, alternating four round full metal jacket, one round tracer. These rounds are fed from a 200-round plastic ammunition box and feed through the side of the weapon. It has a regulator for selecting either normal 750 rpm or the maximum 1,000-rpm rate of fire.

M240 Medium Machine Gun

After extensive operational testing, the U.S. Army selected the M240B medium machine gun as a replacement for the M60 family of machine guns. Manufactured by Fabrique Nationale, the 24.2-pound M240B medium

machine gun is a gas-operated, air-cooled, linked-belt-fed weapon that fires a 7.62x51mm round. The weapon fires from an open-bolt position with a maximum effective range of 1,100 meters. The rate of fire is adjustable from 750 to 1,400 rpm through an adjustable gas regulator. It features a folding bipod, which attaches to the receiver, a quick-change barrel assembly, a feed cover and bolt assembly enabling closure of the cover regardless of bolt position, a plastic buttstock, and an integral optical sight rail. While it possesses many of the same characteristics as the older M60, the durability of the M240 system results in superior reliability and maintainability.

(left) When you have to have suppressive fire and you need a lot of it, the M60A3 is perfect choice. Although over 40 years old, the M60 has undergone numerous modifications, including shortening the weapon and adding a forward grip. Even though it was introduced as a crew-served weapon, an experienced operator can accurately shoulder fire the weapon. This veteran firearm still has a home in the Special Operations community.

(below) After extensive testing, the M240B, manufactured by Fabrique Nationale, was selected as the replacement for the aging M-60 machine gun. The highly reliable 7.62mm machine gun delivers more energy to the target than the smaller caliber M249 SAW. It has an effective range of 1.1 miles with a cyclic rate of fire of 650–950 rpm.

M24 Sniper Weapon System (SWS)

Although Delta has extremely wide latitude in weapons, the current-issue sniper rifle is the M24 SWS. The M24 is based on the Remington 700 series long action. This action accommodates chambering for either the 7.62x51mm or .300 Winchester Magnum round. The rifle is a bolt-action six-shot repeating rifle, (one round in the chamber and five additional rounds in the magazine). It is issued with the Leupold Mark IV 10X M3A scope, commonly referred to as the "Ma-3-Alpha"; additionally, the sniper may make use of the metallic iron sights. Attached to the scope is the M24/EMA ARD (Anti-Reflection Device), a honeycomb of tubes less than three inches long that cuts down the

Mark 11

Knight Manufacturing Company in Florida manufactures the 7.62mm Mark 11 Mod 0 Type Rifle System. It is a highly accurate, precision semi-automatic sniper rifle with a chamber capable of delivering its 7.62mm round well out to 1,000 yards. With a 1/2 inch minute of angle (MOA) accuracy, the Mark 11 has won acceptance in the SOF community as one of the finest semi-automatic sniper rifles in the world. The Mark 11 is based on the

original SR-25; it appears to be an M16 on steroids. In fact, 60 percent of its parts are common to the M16 family. If an operator is familiar with the M16 or M4A1, his hands will naturally fall in place on the Mark 11. From the pistol grip to the safety switch or magazine release, if you've handled an M16 you already know how to operate the Mark 11. The result of this replication is a rifle that is quicker to assimilate, easy to maintain, and more

glare of the scope. The M24 SWS comes with a Harris bipod; however, most of the time the bipod remains in the deployment case. The rifle weighs 12.1 pounds without the scope and has an overall length of 43 inches, with a free-floating barrel of 24 inches. The stock is a composite Kevlar, graphite, and fiberglass with an aluminum-bedding block. The stock has an adjustable buttplate to accommodate the length of pull (LOP).

The M24 Sniper Weapon System was fielded in 1988; prior to this the M21, an adaptation of the M14, was the weapon of choice for sniper teams. The M24 uses the Remington 700 receiver group, an HS Precision stock made from a composite of Kevlar, graphite, and fiberglass bound together with epoxy resins, and features an aluminum-bedding block and adjustable butt plate to accommodate the LOP. This M24 has been painted to further aid the sniper in concealment.

(left) The choice for the SOF sniper when choosing a bolt-action rifle is the M24 SWS, or Sniper Weapon System. Based on a Remington 700 action for 7.62mm, the receiver is adjustable and will take the .300 Winchester Magnum round. It is equipped with a Leupold Mark IV 10X fixed scope referred to as the "Ma-3 Alpha." A detachable bipod, in this case a Harris, can be attached to the stock's fore end. The M24 SWS is a bolt-action rifle capable of engaging a target well over 500 meters.

seamless in transition than any other semi-automatic 7.62mm rifle in the world.

Similar to the M4A1, the Mark 11 has two main sections: the upper and lower receiver. This allows for cleaning in the same manner that the troops have been familiar with since basic training. Another benefit of the receiver's breakdown is the fact that the rifle may be transported in a smaller package for clandestine activities. Once on target,

the rifle is merely reassembled with no effect on the zero of the optics.

The Mark 11 Mod 0 system includes a free-floating 20-inch barrel and a free-floating rail adapter system (RAS). The RAS is similar to the RIS on the M4A1. Another feature of the SR-25 is its ability to mount a sound suppresser. The muzzle blast becomes negligible, and the only sound heard is the sonic crack of the round going downrange.

(left) The Mark 11 Mod 0 Type Rifle System 7.62mm is a highly accurate, precision semi-automatic sniper rifle whose chamber is capable of delivering its 7.62mm round well out to 1,000 yards. *Knight Manufacturing Company /Ichiro Nagata*

(right) When the mission calls for quietly reaching out and touching someone, the Mark 11 has the ability to mount a sound suppresser. The muzzle blast becomes negligible and the only sound heard is the sonic crack of the round going downrange. *Knight Manufacturing Company /Ichiro Nagata*

Heavy Sniper Rifle—The Fifties

When the mission calls for a Hard Target Interdiction (HTI) at very long range (that is, over 1,000 meters), the Delta will turn to the big guns. HTI would be taking out such targets as a generator, an airplane, a helicopter, or another vehicle. The M82A1 is a one-man portable semi-automatic rifle with a magazine holding up to 10 rounds of .50-caliber Browning Machine Gun (BMG) ammunition. The Barrett M107 .50-caliber rifle is currently being fielded. The M107 weighs in at 23 pounds and has a length of 45 inches. It can be reduced in size by further takedown of the weapon, allowing for more covert transport. Using a bullpup design, it is a bolt-action system with a removable 5-round magazine, and is chambered for all NATO .50 caliber BMG cartridges. Other features include a quick-detachable bipod with spiked feet, iron sights, and an M1913 (Picatinny) optical rail to accommodate various sighting and aiming devices. Other .50-caliber weapons common in the armory are those from McMillan as well as others of U.S. and foreign origins.

When hard targets must be engaged over 1,000 meters away, the SF will turn to the Barrett M82A1, semi-automatic .50-caliber rifle. Delta snipers utilized the .50-caliber BMG to knock out the generators at Modelo Prison in Panama when they rescued Kurt Muse. The armory also includes bolt-action, magazine-feed .50-caliber rifles such as the Barrett M107 and McMillan Tac-50.

The dust settles as this team engages the Barrett M82A1 .50-caliber rifle. Capable of engaging target well over 1,500 meters, it is useful against light skin vehicles and aircraft.

AT4

The M136 AT4 is the Army's principal light anti-tank weapon (LAW), providing precision delivery of an 84mm High Explosive Anti-Armor warhead, with negligible recoil. The M136 AT4 is a man-portable self-contained anti-armor weapon, consisting of a free flight, fin-stabilized, rocket-type cartridge packed in an expendable one-piece fiberglass-wrapped tube. Unlike the M72 LAW, the AT4 launcher does not need to be extended before firing. When the warhead makes impact with the target, the nosecone crushes and the impact sensor will activate the internal fuse.

Upon ignition, the piezoelectric fuse element triggers the detonator, initiating the main charge. This results in penetration where the main charge fires and sends the warhead body into a directional gas jet, which is capable of penetrating more than 17 inches of armor plate. The after-effects are "spalling"—the projecting of fragments and incendiary effects generating blinding light and obliterating the interior of the target.

Unlike the M72-series LAW, the AT4 launcher does not need to be extended before firing. With a range of 2,100 meters, the warhead is capable of penetrating 400mm of rolled homogenous armor.

Knives

As with sidearms, Delta operators have wide latitude regarding what knife they may carry. Preferred edged weapons among the operators are the traditional Special Forces favorite the Randall knife, and legendary Gerber blades. From the steamy jungles of Southeast Asia to the vast wasteland of Iraq during Desert Storm, these knives have accompanied many an SF/Delta soldier as he carried out his mission. Selection of an edged weapon is as personal as the operators themselves, and a wide assortment of new and old designed blades can be found. The operator's duffel, load-bearing equipment (LBE), assault vest, or kit bag may contain anything from the standard M9 bayonet to the latest in custom-made combat knives, folding knives from Spyderco and Emerson, or pocket tools like the Leatherman. The Delta operator is as comfortable with a knife—and as lethal—as he is with any firearm.

(center right) While Delta operators have the latest weaponry at their disposal, sometimes the best weapon for the job is an edged weapon. A favorite among the operators is the Randall, Mark I. The Randall is steeped in Special Forces heritage, from the jungles of Vietnam to the desert of Iraq. This Model 1 "All-Purpose Fighting Knife" has a 7-inch blade of 1/4 inch stock. Approximately 3 inches of the top cutting edge is also sharpened. The leather handle is 4 3/4 inches, with a brass double hilt and a Duralumin butt cap.

(lower right) Another favorite knife among the Delta operators is one from the Gerber series. Shown here is the Gerber Mark II, similar to the Fairban-Applegate commando dagger used by the OSS during World War II. This double-edged knife features serrations on both sides of the blade.

(top right) The Gerber Guardian II with scabbard. The Guardian design also features a double-edged blade suitable for sentry removal.

(center right) The M9 Bayonet is the standard-issue bayonet for the U.S. Army and is compatible and inter-changeable with prior designs. Using bayonet lugs, the M9 mounts on the M16A1, M16A2, M4, and M4A1. Features are a 7.125-inch blade, modified wire cutter, T-lug, and blade stop. The scabbard provides the operator with the ability to insert the blade facing either direction, and allows easy attachment/removal from belt. It has black oxide blade coating, weather-resistant zinc phosphate coating on all metal hilt parts, and a Zytel plastic handle.

(left) The M9 bayonet has a slot located near the end of the blade that allows the bayonet to mate with the scabbard. In this configuration, the operator can user the M9 as a wire cutter.

(below) From crimping a blasting cap onto "det cord" to attaching a "PAK4" to a M4A1; whether prying the lid off a demolitions container, or popping the top off the local "brew", this multi-purpose pocket tool kit provides a plethora of uses. Offshoots of the well-known Swiss Army Knife, these tools are available from a wide assortment of manufacturers. Seen here is the Leatherman Wave, which incorporates pliers, knives, screwdrivers, saw blades, and other useful tools.

Demolitions

The M18 Claymore is a directional fragmentation mine containing 700 steel balls and a 1-1/2 pound layer of composition C-4 explosive initiated by a No. 2 electric blasting cap. It measures: 8-1/2 inches long, 1-3/8 inches wide, 3-1/4 inches high, and weighs 3-1/2 pounds. The M18 command-detonated mine may be employed with obstacles or on the approaches, forward edges, flanks, and rear edges of protective minefields as close-in protection against a dismounted infantry attack.

Due to the nature of its missions, Delta Force uses a vast array of demolitions. From small charges to blow the lock off a door to larger charges to take down bridges, operators have the munitions, techniques, and experience to accomplish any mission profile. Delta demolition specialists maintain volumes of data on the most expedient method to employ explosives. How do you blow off a wooden door or a metal door from either a frame building or a concrete bunker? Compiling a comprehensive list of all the explosive and detonation devices available would take volumes, so what follows is a sampling of the munitions in use with Delta.

The M18A1 mine, more commonly referred to as the Claymore mine, is primarily employed as a defensive weapon; however, it has been employed as an offensive weapon in certain situations. The M18A1 can be deployed as a mine, an offensive weapon, or a booby trap; it also has its uses as a pursuit-deterrence device. Additionally, the Claymore has the capability of being sighted directionally to provide fragmentation over a specific target area. It can also be command detonated.

The M18A1 antipersonnel mine is a curved, rectangular plastic case containing a layer of composition C3 explosive. Packed in the explosive on the front face are 700 steel balls, designed to produce an arc-shaped spray, which can be aimed at a predetermined target area. It comes in a bandoleer, which includes the

The Claymore spreads a fan-shaped pattern of steel balls into a 60-degree horizontal arc at a maximum height of 2 meters and covers a casualty radius of 100 meters. The optimum effective range is 50 meters. The forward danger radius for friendly forces is 250 meters. The back blast area is unsafe in unprotected areas 16 meters to the rear and sides of the munition.

M18A1 mine, an M57 firing device, an M40 test set, and an electrical blasting cap assembly.

The M112 block demolition charge consists of 1.25 pounds of Composition C4 packed in an olive drab Mylar-film container with a pressure-sensitive adhesive tape on one surface. A peelable paper cover protects the tape. Composition C4 is white with a unique lemon-citrus smell. The M112 block demolition charge is used primarily for cutting and breaching all types of demolition work. Because of its moldability, the charge is perfectly appropriate for cutting irregularly shaped targets such as steel, steel beams, and so forth. The adhesive backing allows the charge to be attached to any relatively flat, clean, dry surface located above freezing point.

Explosive Breaching covers a diverse selection of explosives and techniques. Explosives such as flexible linear charges, detonation-cord ("det-cord"), and Composition 4 (C4) are all to be found in this demolition repertoire. A common technique used is the silhouette charge: Using a cardboard silhouette with one to three wraps of det-cord around the perimeter will do a good job of cutting through a door. Replace

(above) The M112 block demolition charge is used for an assortment of demolition work. It consists of 1.25 pounds of Composition C4. Composition C4 is white and packed in an olive drab, Mylar-film container, which also aids in concealing the explosive. The M112 block demolition charge can be cut and molded to fit irregularly shaped targets while being easily attached to the target.

(top of page) M700 Time Fuse used for setting timed demolition charges: the fuse is inserted into an M60 Fuse Igniter. Pulling the ring on the M60 releases a striker, which in turn hits the primer, igniting the fuse. The M700 time fuse has a black powder core, which has a burn rate of approximately 1 foot every 40 seconds.

(top left) Blasting caps are available in electric and non-electric and are used for detonating high explosives. Seen here is a M7 nonelectric blasting cap; the flared end allows for the easy insertion of a time fuse.

(middle left) Shown here is an M10 demolition device, filled with Trinitroazetidine (TNAZ). The M10 is extremely useful for sabotage, the device sports various diameter threads allowing the explosive to be screwed into whatever the target may be. A hole on the end facilitates the placement of the blasting cap. Additionally, the device may be pulled apart and the TNAZ utilized for other improvised demolition work.

(middle right) Applying the final touches to a breaching charge. Sticky tape is applied to the center of a silhouette charge, while the outer edge of the cutout has several rows of detonating cord (det-cord) attached. The det-cord consists of a core of high explosive wrapped in a reinforced and waterproof olive drab plastic coating. The core of the det-cord is filled with PETN. *DoD*

(bottom right) The M2 Selectable Lightweight Attack Munition or SLAM. The M2 is self contained, can be easily emplaced and is compatible with other munitions in use in anti-material, anti-vehicular, and anti-personnel. It has four detonation modes: passive IR, magnetic influence, time delay, and command detonation. Weighing a mere 2.2 pounds and small enough to fit in a BDU pocket, it is a low-volume, multipurpose munition.

the det-cord with the proper amount of C4, and the silhouette will now blow out a substantial passageway through a cinder-block wall. Assorted initiators are also taught instant detonation. Whether the need is to breach a brick wall, blow out a door, or take down an enemy bridge, Delta Force has the right demolitions to accomplish the mission. Specialty demolitions called plastic-bonded explosives, or PBX, are available to these covert warriors in an assortment of packages. Plastic-bonded sheet explosives are manufactured with RDX or PETN; they are adaptable, bendable, and as the name implies, a sheet material. Various types of ribbon PBX are available, one such charge for breaching doors and windows and another pliable tape with metal cladding forming a linear-shaped charge, which can be discharged for cutting holes in brick and other masonry walls. Another explosive not normally used by conventional forces is an explosive charge that provides instantaneous breaching, capable of blasting through multiple layers of block walls. The Delta operator is trained for every contingency from wooden-frame to reinforced-steel doors.

Delta teams are always equipped with cutting-edge weaponry and explosive devices, such as the M2 SLAM, or Selectable Lightweight Attack Munitions. The SLAM

Demolitions (continued)

weighs a mere 2.2 pounds, and is small enough to fit in the pocket of a BDU. The explosively formed penetrator (EFP) warhead can penetrate targets of 40mm rolled homogeneous armor out to 25 feet. It has four operating modes: Bottom attack (magnetic influence fuse): As a vehicle passes over the M2, it will sense the magnetic signature and detonate upward; Side attack (passive IR), detonation occurs when sensing a passing vehicle's infrared signature; Timed demolition of a target in four settings, 15, 30, 45, or 60 minutes; and finally, Operator-initiated command detonation, using the standard Army blasting caps or the new-time delay firing device (TDFD).

Another useful explosive device is the M150 Penetration Augmented Munition (PAM). The PAM is a lightweight man-portable demolition device developed for special operations forces. It is compact at 33 inches,

(top right) The M150 Penetration Augmented Munition (PAM) is a lightweight man portable demolition device developed for special operations forces. It is compact at 33 inches, weighs 35 pounds, and can be emplaced by a single Delta operator. The primary use of the demolition device is against reinforced concrete bridge supports, piers, walls, and abutments. *Alliant Techsystem Inc.*

(above) The result of a PAM against a concrete structure. The explosion has fractured the structure and with the result in a loss of 75-degree minimum of the load-bearing capacity. *Alliant Techsystem Inc.*

(right) The shaped demolition charge is a cylindrical block of high explosive. It has a conical cavity in one end that directs the cone lining material into a narrow jet to penetrate materials. This is the 40-pound, M3A1 Shaped Demolition Charge, containing approximately 30 pounds of Composition B. It is capable of penetrating 20 inches of armor plate or 60 inches of reinforced concrete.

weighs 35 pounds, and can be emplaced by a single Delta operator. The primary use of the munition is against reinforced concrete bridge supports, piers, walls, and abutments. The munition can easily be carried in the rucksack or affixed to the soldier's LBE without restricting his ability to walk, climb, rappel, or fast rope. Any standard military detonation device can ignite it.

The PAM is hung against the target. The warhead consists of a forward charge, which cuts any rebar; a hole-drilling charge, which forms a hole in the target; and a follow-through charge, which is propelled to the bottom of the hole it detonates. The explosion fractures the structure and results in a loss of at least 75 percent of the load-bearing capacity. An example would be taking out a bridge: Two operators with two PAM units (70 pounds) could set up the devices and be ready exfil in two minutes. This would contrast with an entire 12-man Special Forces Operational Detachment—Alpha (SF ODA), using 442 pounds of M112 Composition C4 block demolition charge, with a time of 15 minutes per man.

(upper right) This device is packed with C4, creating a shaped explosive charge. For stability it is secured on a tripod. The explosively formed penetrator (EFP) has a Picatinny rail on the top, allowing the attachment of an aiming device, such as the Aimpoint shown here. Once the target has been sighted in, the optical sight is removed and the EFP is set for detonation. The EFP will penetrate a concrete wall or rolled hardened armor.

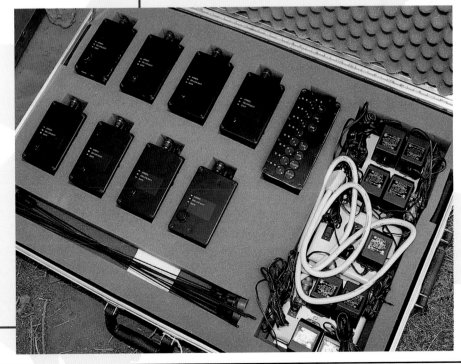

(right) The Radio Firing Device (RFD) kit contains one transmitter, eight receivers with antennas, and battery chargers all in a hard shell carrying case. The Mk186 system is an intelligent and discreet two-way radio-controlled demolition initiation system. The RFD incorporates state-of-the-art microprocessor and encryption technology to provide the operators with a reliable, accurate initiation device that is also compact and safe. Each receiver has the capacity to initiate at least eight M6 electric blasting caps.

Fast Attack Vehicle (FAV)

The FAVs were first introduced into military service in 1980 with the 9th Light Infantry Division the U.S. Army. The program lasted until the mid 1980s. Around this time the U.S. SOF took delivery of a number of the FAVs, and as one of the troops comments, "We began to tinker with them." Today, this modified dune buggy, which now is fitted for three men, is officially called the Desert Patrol Vehicle (DPV), although it also carries the moniker of Light Strike Vehicle and is still referred to as the FAV.

The frame is polyfiber and the cowling can be removed dependent upon the mission profile. Baskets alongside the frame have multiple uses. They can be used for storage of food, water, ammunition, and individuals' gear. Collapsible fuel bladders can also be mounted in the baskets, giving the DPV an extended range for special missions. The baskets can also be used for the recovery of downed pilots. Each DPV can carry out two pilots in the case of CSAR operations.

The DPV has a four-speed transmission, Volkswagen style. However, it is as much a VW as the late Dale Earnhardt's car was a Chevy. The transmission has been highly modified, with only reverse gear being stock. This is because nobody manufactures a reverse racing gear.

The engine is a four-cylinder air-cooled motor. The newer motor in use is now a 20/80cc. It has an internal/external oil cooler on it. This is a big improvement over the FAVs used in Desert Storm. With the new oil cooler, operators can run the DPVs wide open in over 120-degree weather with no problems. The air cleaner is a two-stage system. No matter what conditions it is running in, the first stage stops all the dirt. The crews have never been able to get any dirt out of the second stage of the air cleaner.

specs

FAV
Description: three-man 2x4
Gross DPV weight: 3,500 pounds
Engine Type: Gas (Diesel in development)
Engine Size: 2000 cc
Wheelbase: 114 inches

Overall Length: 161 inches
Overall Height: 79 inches
Overall Width: 83 inches
Ground Clearance: 16 inches
Maximum Grade: 75 percent
Maximum Side Slope: 50 percent

Acceleration: 0 to 30 mph in 4 seconds
Mission Roles: Direct Action, Special Reconnaissance Vehicle, Combat Search and Rescue, Weapons Platform

It has skip plate all along the bottom so rock and similar hazards don't have an effect on the crew or vehicle. Clearance is approximately 16 inches, with 24 inches of wheel travel. The DPV has four shocks in the rear, three of them working all the time. The fourth is the secondary. When the rear wheel travels to a predetermined mileage threshold, it will engage an additional set of torsion bars and the fourth shock. The entire vehicle is tunable by the crew dependent on mission, load, and terrain. The DPV can be set up to carry 2,000 pounds of gear. The seats feature a five-point harness, so the tighter you're strapped in, the better you feel. This way you don't get knocked around too much.

The tires are from Mickey Thompson, and have a bead lock. This allows the DPV to run even on flat tires without the tires coming off the rims. The sidewall also features a tread pattern, so flat or not the tires have traction. Along with the disc brakes, the DPV features cutting brakes. By operating levers, the driver can brake the vehicle and give it a sharp turn. This is extremely useful in an ambush, when the driver needs to maneuver the DPV to get armament lined up on an enemy.

The DPV is bristling with hard points to mount and support various weapons systems. The DPV has two racks for AT-4 (anti-tank missiles), and additional AT-4 can be carried in the side baskets. There is also room in the baskets for Stingers (shoulder-launched surface-to-air missiles). The top mount will accept an M-2 .50-caliber machine gun or Mark 19 40mm grenade launcher. The front mount for the operator riding "Shotgun" normally accepts a 7.62mm light machine gun. The Mark 19 40mm machine-grenade launcher can also be mounted on the vehicle, which gives the crew substantial firepower. With Mark 19s mounted both top and front, the crew of a DPV can put out over 180 rounds downrange in less than 30 seconds. This is often referred to as "steel rain." There is also a rear mount for an M-60A3 or other light machine gun. The primary use for this weapon is to break contact with enemy forces.

(below) It has independent suspension all the way around with four-wheel disc brakes. The suspension is two-stage. On the front end you have the top of the coil spring, which is working all the time. Once this coil is depressed to a predetermined degree, the secondary coil will kick in. This assures a smooth ride throughout the entire range.

(above) Chenowth Racing out of El Cajon, California, manufactors the DPV. According to their spokesman, "It goes anywhere a motorcycle can go and goes where a HUMMV fears to tread!" And go it does! With a speed of more than 60 minutes, the DPV darts across the desert with the ease of a jackrabbit.

(far left) During Operation Desert Storm, Delta Force teams were inserted deep into Iraq with their Fast Attack Vehicles (FAV) to accomplish their mission. These Baja-style dune buggies allowed the operators to conduct Scud hunting operations as well as other yet classified operations.

Tactical Gear

Assault Vests

It began with stuffing extra magazines into BDU pockets, then pouches. As more specialized equipment was added, new LBEs were incorporated into the unit's kit bag. Today, dependent on the mission, the most common way of carrying gear is in the assault vest.

Attached to the pistol belts, the assault vest provides easy access to ammunition and other items during the fast-paced CQB mission. On the front of the vest, pouches may hold magazines for M4A1 5.56mm, MP5 9mm, or 7.62mm, dependent on the weapon of choice for the operator. Small pockets and pouches are readily available to accommodate pistol magazines for .45 or 9mm, shotgun shells, first-aid field dressing, flex cuffs, strobes, chem-lights, pressure dressings, and grenades (including smoke, stun, CS gas, and fragmentation). Some vest designs have a modular nature, with the vest made up of attachment points via Velcro, Alice clips, or other fasteners. These systems allow for the modification of

The PRC-137 is an ultra lightweight HF radio unique to U.S. SOF. Using a small keyboard, the operator types in the message to be sent; it is then downloaded into the radio. He may then continue on his mission. When the base station comes online, an automatic link will be established with the PRC-137 and the message will be uploaded.

the user's vest with assorted holsters, magazine pouches, radio pockets, and so on. Internal pockets allow the operators to stow maps or other gear. Additionally, these vests may have various-sized back pouches to accommodate such items as gas masks, helmets, demolition equipment, and other mission-essential items.

The team's SOP will determine the layout of the vest. For example, "like-teams," entry teams, breaching teams, clearing teams, sniper teams, and so on are configured similarly. All team members are sure of each other's equipment capabilities, equipment is exchangeable, training continuity is achievable, and less variation in team equipment means fewer problems to consider. Another requisite item worn on the vests will be the U.S. flag. The practice of wearing flags dates back to Desert One in 1980, when flags were sewn onto the shoulders of the uniforms and covered with 100 mile-per-hour tape. Today the national ensigns are Velcro backed and attached to the vest as well as the uniform. On deployments the flag is depicted as flying forward.

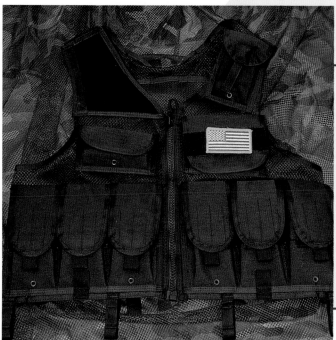

(above) Having performed their raid, this team exits the building. They can be seen with various Assault Vest configurations. Setup of the vest may vary from team to team, but each individual will know where to find an item on his buddy's vest should the need arise. Often you'll find flash bang grenade pouches on the back of the operator, readily available should the need arise. *DoD*

(left) Assault Vests are common among Delta; this vest is manufactured by Eagle Industries. These vests allow the operators to keep necessary tactical equipment within reach at a moment's notice—when seconds mean the difference between life and death. Attached to the pistol belts, assault vests provide an easy access to ammunition and other items during the fast-paced CQB mission.

Assault Vests (continued)

(right) This photo shows an M9 Beretta in a tactical holster. Most operators will opt to carry their sidearms in what is called a drop-down holster; Attaching to the pistol belt with an extension hanger places the holster just above the knee. The benefit of this style of holster is that allows greater stability and ease of access in combat situations.

(below) This vest also features two cavernous back pouches to accommodate such items as gas masks, helmets, demolition equipment, and other mission essential items.

(left) The Delta Operator Assault vest (DOAV), manufactured by Black Hawk Industries, features pouches to hold magazines for the missions weapon of choice. Smaller pockets and pouches are accessible for pistol magazines, shotgun shells, flex cuffs, strobes, chem-lights, first aid pressure dressings, and grenades, (including smoke, stun, CS gas, and frags. The DOAV also has internal pockets, giving the operator storage for maps and other equipment.

Night Vision Equipment

The AN/PVS-7 is a single-tube night-vision goggle (NVG), Generation III/Omni IV image intensifier that employs prisms and lenses to provide the operator with simulated binocular vision. The AN/PVS-7 contains a high light-level-protection circuit in a passive, self-contained image intensifier device, which amplifies existing ambient light to provide the operator a means of conducting night operations.

AN/PVS-14 Night Vision Monocular may be worn on a head-mount assembly, mounted on the U.S. Military PAGST Kevlar combat helmet, or mounted directly on the operator's weapon. The mount incorporates adjustments front and back and flip-up/flip-down capability. An optional three-power (3X) focal-magnifier

The AN/PVS-7 is a lightweight, high-performance passive third-generation image intensifier system. Using these night vision goggles (NVG) turns the night into day. The NVG unit is self-contained night vision system containing one binocular unit consisting of an objective lens assembly, an image intensifier tube, a housing assembly, and a binocular eyepiece assembly. The PVS7 can be worn on a head mounting assembly, around the operator's neck for instant use, or stashed away in the assault vest. To aid in close proximity viewing, the NVG has an infrared (IR) light source, which provides illumination. Seen here is a soldier wearing AN/PVS-7 NVGs; he is armed with an M4A1 carbine equipped with AN/PEQ-2 IR laser aiming device and 4X ACOG scope.

AN/PVS-14 is the optimum night vision monocular for special applications. It can be used hand held, on a facemask, helmet-mounted, or attached to the RIS/RAS of a weapon. The AN/PVS-14 manufactured by ITT offers the latest, state-of-the-art capability in a package that meets the rigorous demands of the U.S. Military's SOF. By using the monocular configuration the user can operate with night vision, while maintaining night vision in the opposite eye.

Night Vision Equipment (continued)

(far right) The AN/PVS-21 Low Profile/Night Vision Goggle uses patented folded optical systems for a low profile NVG with see-through capability. The two image intensifier tubes are positioned vertically rather than horizontally. The two objective lenses are situated at cheek level on each side of the face. This placement provides a low center of gravity, thus eliminating neck fatigue and reducing the possibility of entangling the goggles with other objects. *Special Technology Systems*

(below) The AN/PVS-21 is a Gen III OMNI IV system. The unique see-through capabilities allow the operator to observe the scene simultaneously using the direct view and the intensified view. This eliminates the tunnel vision found on other NVGs. Wearing the LP/NVGs, the operator can shoulder fire a weapon accurately with conventional optics or IR laser pointers. The system may also be used for HALO or static line parachute operations. *Special Technology Systems*

lens assembly is designed to temporarily attach to the objective lens for long-range viewing. Similar to the AN/PVS7 NVGs, an optional magnetic compass module can be attached to the AN/PVS-14, providing an easily read magnetic heading in the field of view.

AN/PVS-21 Low Profile NVG were designed to meet the needs of the operators for stealth and aggressive night-vision operations. The PVS-21 LP/NVGs features three characteristics unique to these goggles: 1. they use "folded optics," 2. they have an innovative see-through capability, and 3. they have a built-in Heads-Up-Display (HUD) that provides the operator with matchless versatility.

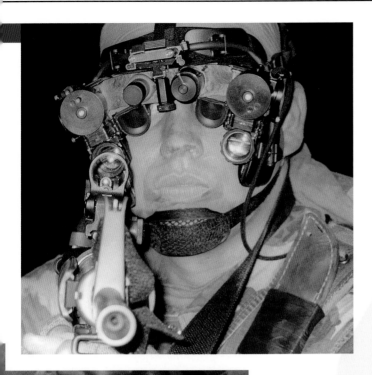

Radios

Communications is the lifeline of any Delta team on a mission. From miniature satellite phones with encryption to standard SOF-issue radios, a Delta operation is only a short call away from JSOC. For long-range communications, the AN/PSC-5 (V) "Shadowfire" by Raytheon is used. The PSC-5 is a multi-band, multi-mission communication terminal with capability for UHF/VHF (Ultra High Frequency/Very High Frequency) man-pack LOS (Line-Of-Sight) and satellite communications (SATCOM). For satellite communications, the set provides both TDMA, (Time Division Multiple Access) and DAMA (Demand Assigned Multiple Access). This device supports the Department of Defense (DOD) requirement for a lightweight, secure, network-capable, multi-band, multi-mission, anti-jam, voice/imagery/data communication capability in a single package.

For tactical intra-team communications, the teams will be issued the Multi-Band Inter/Intra Team Radios, which provide the teams with the ability to communicate on user-selected frequencies from 30 to 512 MHz utilizing a single hand-held radio. Up to 5 watts are available in VHF/FM, VHF/AM, UHF/AM, and UHF/FM(LOS) for ground-to-ground and air-to-ground connectivity. Weighing only 31 ounces, it has two versions immersible

Communications is the lifeline of any of the SOF and Delta is no exception. Seen here is the AN/PSC-5 (V) "Shadowfire" by Raytheon. The Shadowfire weighs 11.7 pounds without the battery; adding the power-supply, the weight goes up 8 pounds. It is UHF/VHF, Line-Of-Sight, and SATCOM capable.

Radios (continued)

to 6 feet and 66 feet. The units are embedded Communications Security (COMSEC) for full digital voice and data operations.

Thales Communication Multiband Inter/Intra Team Radio (MBITR) is a powerful tactical handheld radio designed for the USSOCOM. The MBITR more than meets the tough SOCOM requirements and provides a secure voice and digital-data radio with exceptional versatility, ruggedness, and reliability.

The immersible unit weighs less than 2 pounds and includes a keypad, graphics display, and built-in speaker-microphone. Typical of the advanced designs of Thales radios, MBITR employs digital-signal processing and flash memory to support functions traditionally performed by discrete hardware in other manufacturers' equipment. The power output is up to 5 watts over the 30–512-MHz frequency band. The MBITR has embedded Type 1 COMSEC for both voice and data traffic.

The ICOM IC-F3 is a hand-held VHF transceiver. ICOM also manufactures a UHF transceiver designated the IC-F4. These units provide unit-to-unit communications and varying levels of priorities. The ICOM radios provide the basis for the Solider Intercom to fill the requirement for an infantry inter-squad radio. It can be used with an assortment of headsets providing a low threat exposure and stealth operation for the operators. *ICOM*

Thale's Multiband Inter/Intra Team Radio (MBITR) is a powerful tactical handheld radio designed for the U.S. Special Operations Command. Designated the AN/PRC148, it provides a secure voice and digital-data radio with exceptional versatility, ruggedness, and reliability. This immersible unit weighs less than 2 pounds and includes a keypad, graphics display, and built-in speaker-microphone. The MBITR has embedded Type 1 COMSEC for both voice and data traffic. Attached to the MBITR is a H-250/U Sonetronics Handset, which provides dynamic noise canceling allowing the operator to communicate clearly.

Thales' Miniature Secure Handheld Radio (MSHR) sets the standard for tactical radio design, with an amazing amount of capability packed into the world's smallest secure digital radio: a small but tough package. It features true digital design, flash memory, Type 1 (or exportable) encryption, and is endorsed by the National Security Agency (NSA). It has voice and secure digital data, narrowband capability—yet it's just half the size and weight of other radios in the military's inventory.

Motorola is no stranger when it comes to U.S. Special Operations in general and Delta Force in particular. During the Iranian rescue mission, Delta operators were equipped with Motorola URC-101/101 radios. From suitcase SATCOMs to secure personalized radios, the Motorola Company has been involved with many Delta missions. Their support in making operations successful is paramount in the industry. One of their latest contributions, the ASTRO SABER, is presented on the following page.

(right) The Miniature Secure Handheld Radio (MSHR) manufactured by Thales Communication, Inc. is the world's smallest secure digital radio. It features true digital design, flash memory, embedded US Type 1 encryption, and is endorsed by the National Security Agency (NSA). Weighing in at only 18 ounces, it features secure voice and data modes and is water immersible to 1 meter.

(lower right) The LASH unit can be set up with a Push-To-Talk (PTT) body or hand switch (suitable for snipers). Usable in a wide range of environments, it is not affected by loud ambient sounds. Wearing the LASH, the team can communicate one to another in tones so low they are inaudible to another person standing 24 inches away.

(below) The LASH radio headset has been the mainstay of CT teams for many years. Mounted around the operator's neck, the throat microphone picks up the vibration of the voice box. It can transmit a whisper as if the team were talking in normal voices.

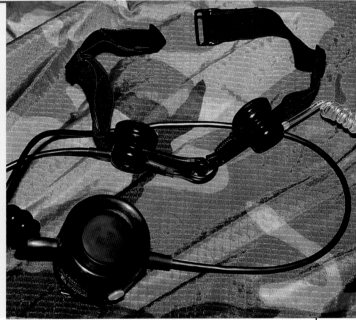

Radios (continued)

ASTRO SABER digital technology delivers consistent audio quality throughout the operator's coverage area. This technology provides enhanced signaling and control, greater spectral efficiency, and a full range of encryption capabilities. It is a full-functional digital portable radio with the flexibility to work in both digital and analog environments. Individual users can custom program commonly used or critical features on a radio-by-radio basis through programmable buttons and soft-key access. A ruggedized version is available for use in demanding environments such as heat, vapor, or saltwater.

(left) A "Ruggedized" ASTRO SABER Digital Radio by Motorola. Saber radios are compatible with a full array of Motorola's current analog systems, including Conventional STAT-Alert, SECURENET systems, SMARTNET Type II and Smart Zone trunked systems digital technology. It delivers consistent voice quality throughout the operator's coverage area, enhanced signaling and control, greater spectral efficiency, and improved secure communications. Digital solutions are available in VHF, UHF, and 800 MHz frequencies for both conventional and trunked applications with enhanced encryption, COMSEC US Type 1.

(below) The TASC II unit can be configured in a wide assortment of boom or throat microphones. The earpiece assembly is manufactured with either a splashproof or waterproof speaker.

The pliable rubber ear cup of the TASC II establishes contact with the operator's head to lessen ambient sounds. The headset has an adjustable elastic strap, allowing the user to comfortably wear the device, whether fast roping, moving under fire, or even swimming.

(below) This photo shows the LITE headset. Its streamlined design makes it perfect for fitting under ballistic helmets, or under a gas mask. The boom microphones can instantly be transitioned to a mask microphone when the team employs CS or other types of gas. The unit has vents in the earpiece allowing the operator to pick up on ambient sounds. The unit is weatherproof and can be configured with an assortment of PTT switches.

One of the various PTT switches for the LITE radio headset.

(top right) The INVISIO Bone-mic Headset is a complete headset that fits inside the ear of the operator while a special earpiece rests on the bone in front of the ear. The INVISIO utilizes a special shock absorber that makes close contact with the user's jawbone. The sound waves will actually vibrate through the bone and the operator will hear as clearly as if the earpiece were placed in the ear. This system is extremely effective in a high noise environment since the body of the user protects the microphone.

(left) The Eagle Special Operations/Low Profile Headset can be configured in a single or dual bone-vibrating audio transducer. This configuration provides the operator with precise, clear, and discreet reception of incoming radio traffic. Radio signals are transferred to the inner ear cochlea through the facial bones, thus allowing both ears open for ambient hearing. This state-of-the-art headset is rugged, lightweight, and low profile. The unit fits close to the user's face, allowing it to be easily worn under ballistic helmets, gas masks, and balaclavas.

Global Positioning System (GPS)

While all Delta operators excel in land navigation using the standard-issue Lensetic Compass, it is equally important for the teams to be able to have pinpoint accuracy when conducting a DA mission through the desert, across the frozen tundra, or in enemy territory in the middle of the night. They will need to know the position of a terrorist's hideout, a radar station, or perhaps a SCUD when reporting in to headquarters. In such instances they will use a device known as a Global Positioning System, or GPS.

The Global Positioning System is a collection of satellites that orbit the earth twice a day. During their orbits they transmit the precise time, latitude, longitude, and altitude information. Using a GPS receiver, special operations forces can ascertain exact locations anywhere on the earth.

Utilizing Global Positioning System (GPS), Delta operators were able to determine their positions accurately to carry out their variety of missions across the wasteland of the Iraqi desert during the Gulf War. Here it is seen in a vehicular mount inside a HUMMV.

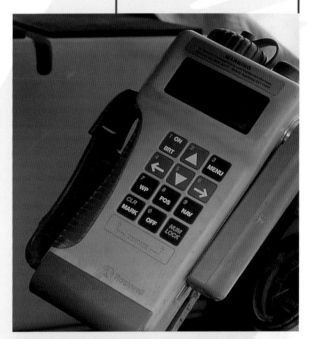

The Rockwell Precision Lightweight GPS Receiver, or PLGR+96, referred to as the "Plugger," will continuously track up to five satellites. The unit is sealed for operations in all environments, and accurately computes position coordinates, elevation, speed, and time data from transmitted signals from the Navstar GPS satellites.

In the event the team would be compromised, they can zero the unit so no data is available for the enemy. All data, waypoints, and so on are reset to zero.

global positioning system

The Global Positioning System (GPS) was developed by the U.S. Department of Defense in the early 1970s to provide a continuous worldwide positioning and navigational system for U.S. military forces around the globe. The complete constellation, as it is referred to, consists of 24 satellites orbiting approximately 12,000 miles above the earth. These 22 active and two reserve, or back-up, satellites provide data 24 hours a day for 2D and 3D positioning anywhere on the planet. Each satellite constantly broadcasts the precise time and location data. Troops using a GPS receiver receive these signals. The greater the number of satellites and the more dynamic the positions, the more precisely the system can determine the person's location.

By measuring the time interval of the transmission and the receiving of the satellite signal, the GPS receiver calculates the distance between the users and each satellite. Using the distance measurements of at least three satellites in an algorithm computation, the GPS receiver provides the precise location. Using a special encryption signal results in Precise Positioning Service (PPS), which is used by the military. A second signal called Standard Positioning Service (SPS) is available for civilian and commercial use.

The current GPS unit is the Rockwell "Plugger," or PSN-11. The precise name for the unit is PLGR96 (Precise Lightweight GPS Receiver). The PLGR96 is the most advanced version of the U.S. Department of Defense handheld GPS unit. It addresses the increasingly demanding requirements of the Delta, as well as all of the U.S. SOF.

Secure (Y-code) Differential GPS (SDGPS) allows the user to accept differential correction without zeroing the unit. Differential accuracy can be less than one meter. Other features of the Plugger include: Wide Area GPS Enhancement (WAGE) for autonomous positioning accuracy to four meters, jammer direction finding, targeting interface with laser range-finder, remote display terminal capability, and advanced user interface features.

Weighing in at a mere 2.7 pounds (with batteries installed), the GPS unit is easily stowed in the cavernous rucksack or even in a pocket of the Delta operator's assault vest. In addition to handheld operation, the PLGR96 unit can be installed into various vehicles and airborne platforms.

For missions that require the operators to infiltrate underwater, there is the Miniature Underwater Global Positioning System Receiver (MUGR). This small device, weighing a mere 1.2 pounds, provides the team with positioning and navigational information needed for Infil/Exfil, fire support, DA, and target location. Once the unit acquires the satellite fix, the waterproof MUGR can be taken to a depth of 33 feet. Alternately, the unit may work under water using the optional floating antenna.

SOFLAM

The Special Operations Forces–Laser Acquisition Marker (SOFLAM) is utilized in a direct action mission (DAM) for the direction of terminal-guided ordnance (TGO). This technique is referred to as "lasing the target." When it absolutely, positively has to be destroyed, you put a team on the ground and a fast mover with a smart bomb in the air. Result: one smoking bomb crater. This newly issued laser-marking device is lighter and more compact than the current laser marker currently in service with the U.S. military. It provides the operators with the capability to locate and designate critical enemy targets for destruction by laser-guided ordnance. It can be utilized in daylight or employed at night with the attached night vision optics.

SOFLAM is a lightweight, compact, man-portable laser target designator and rangefinder. Using the 10X optics of the SOFLAM enables operators to direct terminal guided ordnance, that is, "smart weapons" such as Paveway bombs, Hellfire missiles, and Copperhead munitions. The unit weighs in at slightly less than 12 pounds and has a range out to 10 Kilometers.

Additional Gear

(right) When the mission calls for dynamic entry, the Delta team may employ a specialized hand grenade. The XM84 Stun Grenade is a non-fragmentation and non-lethal stun grenade. Known as a Flash/Bang, its intended function is to provide the entry team with a consistent and effective means of neutralizing any terrorist threat. The bright flash and deafening explosion disorients any enemy personnel, allowing the operators the tactical edge in eliminating any hostiles. *Universal Propulsion*

(below) The standard issue Strobe and IR cover carried by Delta operators. While common among all U.S. SOF, the strobe is useful to facilitate air-traffic-control (ATC) and other ground to air signaling. Operators may also attach them to their helmets when performing HALO/HAHO jumps to ID team members. Shown here with the IR cover, which is visible using NVGs.

"Have thrown smoke, identify." While Delta troops are equipped with the latest high tech equipment, the venerable smoke grenade has its place in the rucksacks and assault vests of these elite troopers. It is not unusual to find a smoke grenade or two stashed away in an operator's rucksack or assault vest for signaling positions, or marking as HLZ for pickup. M18 Colored Smoke grenade (left shoulder) comes in red, green, yellow, and violet. The grenade produces a cloud of colored smoke for 50 to 90 seconds.

(right) The Phoenix IR transmitter, weighing a scant 2 ounces, is a pocketsize user-programmable IR beacon designed for personal combat identification, (CID). Invisible to the naked eye, when observed with NVG it can be seen up to 20 miles away. A 9-volt battery, lightweight and easy to use, powers the transmitter. The Phoenix Jr. is a simple on/off strobe. The other unit contains two protruding pins, allowing the unit to be programmed with a varying series of patterns.

(below) Delta draws from the ranks of Special Forces; hence they will have their share of SF Medical Sergeants. Trained in a vast array of first aid and trauma medicine, their skills are second only to the MDs and surgeons assigned to the Force. Even though he is a medical specialist, he is also a combatant and is fully capable of treating a gunshot wound, or "taking out" a terrorist.

Additional Gear (continued)

An inside look at an 18Delta's medical pack. These trauma bags are packed with an assortment of medical supplies, all within easy reach to perform the necessary medical treatment: bandaging, intubations, splints, chest tubes, tracheotomy kit, IV setups, medications, and so on. The bags are loaded and carried in accordance with mission parameters.

As with other equipment, Delta operators are given wide latitude in eye protection. These tactical goggles are the Bolle Commando model. It is a multi-purpose goggle that provides protection from fragments, sand, dust, and so forth. The goggle is a foamless system, which allows the goggles to seal to the operator's face.

The Bolle Attacker goggle is another choice for tactical use. Favored among many of the counterterrorst units, they can be found in the kit bags of the Delta operators. The Attacker goggles feature foam, which moulds to the operator's face or, as seen here, his balaclava.

While the Force is equipped with the most lethal weaponry, they also employ low-tech equipment. Here a trooper is seen wearing kneepads, which provide protection when he has to "hit the dirt," or rapidly navigate through a building. These hard plastic outers are foam lined and have open slots in the back to allow extra padding. Elbow pads are often employed as well. This trooper is armed with an MP5, commo headset, and heavily-laden rucksack.

As most of their missions depend on stealth and secrecy, there is more probability of operators banging their heads on a helicopter airframe or stairwell than getting shot. With this in mind, operators often wear Pro-Tec Helmets during missions to provide protection to their most lethal weapon, their mind. The helmet on the left is the side-cut model allowing unrestricted hearing, while the helmet on the right is a full-cut model. A PVS-7 NVG rests between the two models.

Additional Gear (continued)

(left) The CamelBak hydration system is a plastic water bladder connected to a length of hose. It fits into an insulated bag that can be strapped on the carrier's back or attached to a rucksack. The hose is positioned close to the wearer's shoulder strap to eliminate snagging on obstacles. Since the water does not slosh, it is silent.

(below) HydraStorm is a hydration system offered by Blackhawk Industries, who states it is "designed and manufactured by operators for operators!" Hydra Storm provides an integrated system that works with a soldier. Weighing two pounds per canteen, the operator will normally have two canteens attached to his pistol belt, which can be awkward to carry and access. Wearing the HydraStorm on the back, the bite valve is readily available and can be accessed on the move without fumbling around for a canteen and canteen cover.

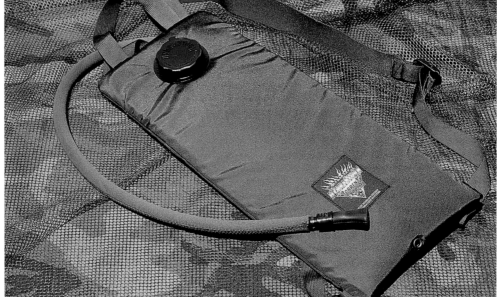

(above) Delta casual: for times when the mission calls for low profile, the operators abandon their BDUs for Polo shirts and Levis. Wide latitude, personal preference, and mission parameters may find some of the following gear in the kit bags. Banana Republic vest, and (clockwise) small binoculars, carabiners, HK .45 caliber pistol, extra magazine, Mini-Maglight flashlight, Invisio Ear-Bone Mic, Leatherman Wave multipurpose tool, Saber radio, ASP expandable baton, and Emerson CQC7 Close Quarters Combat folding knife.

(left) Delta members wear the US-ASOC shoulder patch. The insignia is red with a black unsheathed dagger, which denotes absolute military preparedness.

Techniques

While Delta may be called upon for a variety of missions, its forte is CT/CQB operations usually involving a hostage, POW, or other "precious cargo" in the hands of terrorists or other hostile forces. The operators' extensive training places an emphasis on advanced marksmanship and close-proximity shooting; ballistic, mechanical, and explosive breaching techniques for doors, windows, and walls; building, climbing, and rappelling procedures; Fast Rope techniques; CQB in multi-team and multi-breach points, along with multi-story and multi-building environments. Delta operators will conduct training exercises engaging linear targets, such as buses, trains, and airplanes. Where is the best place to enter a hijacked train? How fast can they get into that bus before the terrorists

Fast Rope Insertion/Extraction System or FRIES, as seen here from this MH-47. A four-man Delta team can be inserted within 5-7 seconds. Once over the insertion point, the rope is deployed and even as it is hitting the ground the operators are jumping onto the woolen line and sliding down as easily as a fireman slides down a pole. This team is armed with M4A1 carbines.

(above) A "stack" prepares for dynamic entry into a building. The operators will conduct a breach, enter the building, clear the room, collapse on their sector, and secure the structure. Elapsed time from breach will take an average of 4 seconds. That is less time than it took to read this caption.

(left) Task Force Ranger in Somalia drove the point home that MOUT, or Military Operations in Urban Terrain, is deadly. Moving across intersections, courtyards, alleys, and house-to-house brings with it a new set of challenges. With much of the world's conflicts centering on highly-populated areas, no matter how primitive, the teams must adapt, overcome, and improvise to meet the demands of urban combat. With the building secure, and security posted, the team prepares to exit a building and Exfil the area.

start harming the hostages? How much movement will be noticed if the fuel in the airplane's wing tank is not full? All the questions are presented, answered, evaluated, and reviewed again. All contingencies are addressed, options discussed, and missions rehearsed until they are perfect. Once this point has been reached, the operators continue to use their imagination, to think outside the box: What if . . .? Suppose we do this . . .? Then they build in the contingencies for the what-ifs.

"Reach out and touch someone" brings on an entirely new meaning when it involves "taking out" an enemy sentry. Sometimes this means using a suppressed weapon, or in this case a Gerber BMF knife, which is used to demonstrate the appropriate method of dispatching an enemy sentry.

(center right) Known as the Australian Peel, this method of breaking contact with the enemy is an effective technique employing cover and movement. The basic principle of this procedure follows: upon initial contact everyone hits the ground engaging direct fire into the attacking force. The lead men collapse back through a corridor created by their teammates, who are laying down suppressive fire. Reloading their weapons as they move, they are prepared to hit the ground and provide cover fire as the rest of the team to collapses on them.

(bottom right) The time comes when you need to break contact with the enemy; Cover and Movement best achieve this. If you want to see an example of this, view the movie *Heat;* there is a scene showing this technique. Sources have indicated former Delta operators were on the set as technical advisers for the scene.

(above) There is no better sniper in the world than a Delta sniper. Delta snipers learn their trade at the Special Operations Target Interdiction Course (SOTIC), at Ft. Bragg, North Carolina. SOTIC, better known as Sniper Training, is a Level 1 category course for U.S. Special Operations Forces. Level 1 in simple terms means a SOTIC sniper can drop an enemy if he is standing right next to you. The capability of employing such precision sniper fire is extremely useful in CT/Hostage missions.

(left) A sniper and his spotter pose slightly out of the brush, so we can see their "ghille" suits. This is a view an enemy will never see; the last thing that will be going through the enemy's mind is a 7.62mm, 168grain, Boat Tail Hollow Point.

A High Altitude Low Opening (HALO) parachute jumper suited up and ready to go. HALO is one of the means by which teams can be inserted into denied or hostile territory. Jumpers are capable of exiting an aircraft at 25,000 feet using oxygen; they will then freefall to a designated altitude where they will deploy the Ram Air Parachute System (RAPS) and form up together. *Defense Visual Information Center*

HALO/HAHO

There are times when, for political reasons or strategic or tactical considerations, a team cannot just drop into an enemy's backyard. You must insert your team clandestinely from afar and outside of the nation's territorial airspace or boundaries. For such an insertion a U.S. Special Operations team would use either High Altitude Low Opening (HALO) or High Altitude High Opening (HAHO).

These types of parachute operations will be flights over or adjacent to the objective area from altitudes not normally associated with conventional static-line parachuting. HALO/HAHO infiltrations are normally conducted under the cover of darkness or at twilight to lessen the chance of observation by hostile forces. Using the Ram Air Parachute System (RAPS), operators deploy their parachutes at a designated altitude, assemble in the air, and land together in the arranged drop zone (DZ) to begin their mission. This type of drop can be conducted even in adverse weather conditions.

Flying at an altitude of 25,000 to 43,000 feet MSL (mean sea level) the jump aircraft, such as a MC-130H Combat Talon, will appear as legitimate aircraft on an enemy's radar screen, perhaps just another commercial airliner traversing the globe. What the radar operator will not know is that the aircraft is the launching platform for the world's most lethal CT system—a team of highly trained Delta operators.

Military free-fall (MFF) operations are ideally adapted for the infiltration of Delta teams. While the maximum exit altitude is 43,000 feet MSL, MFF operations may be as low as 5,000 feet above ground level (AGL). A typical team can be deployed in a fraction of the time it would take for a conventional static-line jump. Normal opening altitudes range from 3,500 AGL to 25,000 MSL, dependent on mission parameters.

As the AFSOC pilots approach the insertion point, the ramp of the MC-130H will lower. With the combination of aircraft noise, the MFF parachutist helmet,

Here a HALO jumper floats down to earth using the RAPS. This jumper is prepared to drop his rucksack, which is suspended by webbing straps. Note the M4 rifle tucked along his left side. "Airborne, All The Way!" All Delta Force operators are Airborne qualified.

Seen here is an alternative to attaching the rucksack in the front of the jumper. This HALO jumper is wearing the ruck behind his legs, under the parachute. In some cases, this is personal preference; in others it is team Standard Operating Procedure (SOP).

MAX. WT.
1100 LBS/FT2
ON THIS COVER

HALO/HAHO (continued)

and the wearing of an oxygen mask, any normal verbal communication is almost impossible. For this reason the team will communicate with the use of arm and hand signals or inter-team radios. Having already received the signals to don helmets, unfasten seat belts, and check oxygen, the jumpmaster waits for the team to signal back "O.K."

Approximately 2 minutes before the insertion, the jumpmaster raises his arm upward from his side indicating the team should stand up. Next he extends his arm straight out at shoulder level, palm up, then bends it to touch his helmet, indicating "move to the rear." The insertion team equipped with ram air parachutes, oxygen masks, and goggles stands up and gets ready to jump. If jumping from the side jump door, the lead man will be a meter away; if going out the rear of the plane, he will stop at the hinge of the cargo ramp. With their rucksacks or combat assault vests loaded with mission-essential equipment, the parachutists head toward the rear of the plane. Moments turn into an eternity and then it is time: As the aircraft reaches the proper coordinates for the drop, the jump light emits a steady green. The command is given: "Go!" In a matter of seconds the team heads down the ramp and out into the darkness as the drone of the plane's engines fades off into the distance.

Depending on the mission parameters, the team will perform a HALO or HAHO jump. In HALO, the team will exit the plane and free fall through the airspace, meeting up at a prearranged time or altitude. Jumping in this manner, the team appears so small that its members are virtually invisible to the naked eye and, of course, will not show up on any enemy radar screen. Using GPS units and altimeters, the team will descend until fairly close to the drop zone. At that point they will open their chutes and prepare for the very short trip to the ground.

The alternate method, HAHO, is jumping from an extreme height with oxygen. The difference is that as soon as the team jumps off, the members immediately deploy their parachutes and use them to glide into a denied area. For this type of jump, they also utilize GPS units and altimeters. In order to maintain formation integrity, each jumper has a strobe on his helmet (either normal or IR) and the team wears the appropriate NVGs. Additionally, each man on the team is on inter-

team radio for command and control of the insertion, as well as formation on the DZ.

There are a number of advantages to employing the HALO/HAHO procedures. There are times when, due to the presence of enemy air defenses, it is the best means to infiltrate a team into a hostile area; this also increases the survivability of the support aircraft. If the mission requires the team to jump into a mountainous terrain where it would not be practical or prudent to attempt a static-line parachute operation, MFF would be a practical option. Other benefits include times when navigational aids (NAVAIDS) are not available to guarantee the requisite precision of drops at low altitudes, such as, deserts or jungle environments. These would be times it is deemed necessary to land the team at multiple points of an objective for the purpose of attacking or seizing a primary target, and the mission success requires a low-signature infiltration.

Military Free Fall or HALO training is conducted at Ft. Bragg and Yuma Proving Grounds. The SOF trooper is wearing a Gentex helmet with oxygen in place and is armed with a Colt M4 rifle. This jumper has attached his rucksack to the front of his harness; an alternative would be to mount the ruck behind his legs.

FRIES

(above) FRIES, the fastest method of inserting a team. Here a team inserts from a U.S. Air Force MH-53 Pave Low. Unlike rappelling, once the trooper hits the ground, he is "free" of the rope and can begin his mission. These shooters are equipped with MP5 submachine guns. *Defense Visual Information Center*

(below) A single rope is lowered from the hovering helicopter. Wearing a special harness, the team member(s) are attached to the rope via snap links. Once secure to the line, the helicopter will whisk them out of harm's way.

Fast Rope Insertion/Extraction System (FRIES) is used to "insert" an assault force onto the ground in seconds. This system begins with small woven ropes made of wool, which are then braided into a larger rope. The rope is rolled into a deployment bag and the end secured to the helicopter. Depending on the model of chopper, it can be just outside on the hoist mechanism of the side door or attached to a bracket off the back ramp. Once over the insertion point, the rope is deployed and, even as it is hitting the ground, the Delta Operators are jumping onto the woolen line and sliding down—as easily as a fireman goes down a pole. Once the team is safely on the ground, the flight engineer or gunner—depending on the type of helicopter—pulls the safety pin, and the rope falls to the ground. Such a system is extremely useful in the rapid deployment of Delta personnel; an entire assault team can be inserted within 10 to 15 seconds. FRIES is the most accepted way to get a force onto the ground expeditiously. Unlike rappelling, once the

FRIES (continued)

trooper hits the ground, he is free of the rope and can begin his mission.

The second part of FRIES is the "extraction" method. Originally referring to it as SPIES or Special Procedure, Insertion & Extraction System, the Army has combined both methods into one term. While fast roping gets you down quickly, there are times when you have to extract just as fast. The problem is, there is no landing zone (LZ) for the Blackhawk of the 160th SOAR(A) to land, and the "bad guys" are closing in on your position. This technique is similar to the McGuire and STABO rigs developed during the Vietnam War. Both used multiple ropes, which often resulted in the troops colliding. The latter at least had the benefit of allowing the user to employ his weapon while on the ride up. What served the Special Forces troops of the 1960s has been refined to the new FRIES method.

While the technique has changed, the methodology remains. A single rope is lowered from the hovering helicopter. Attached to this rope are rings, woven

Rappelling is still an available technique utilized by the Delta troops whether abseiling down the side of a building or the side of a mountain. The technique offers more control than the FRIES system. Unlike the FRIES, the operator is able to have a free hand to facilitate firing a weapon, or tossing a flash/bang through a window opening.

(left) The second part of FRIES is the extraction method. Originally referred to as SPIES or Special Procedure, Insertion & Extraction System, the Army has combined both methods. While fast roping gets you down quickly, there are times when you have to extract just as fast. *Defense Visual Information Center*

(above) A "rubber duck" is the term used to describe a mission where there is a need to deploy a Zodiac raft. There is the Soft Duck, where a fully inflated Zodiac raft is deployed from the rear cargo ramp of a "Night Stalker" MH-47E Chinook, or an AFSOC MH-53 Pave Low. The raft is slid out of the back of the helicopter and the team follows right behind.

(left) Rubber Duck operations from an MH-47E. Immediately after the Zodiac raft has cleared the ramp, the team will follow it out. Swimming to the raft they will then load in, start the outboard motor, and continue their insertion to their target area.

(right) "Mission complete. Request Exfil." The Delta Queen is a method for retrieval and extraction of an SOF team. When it is time to Exfil, the team will return to the Zodiac and head for the extraction point. The team will meet up with an MH-47E Chinook of the 160th SOAR(A). The pilot will bring his aircraft to a hover, and then bring the helicopter down, closer and closer to the water's surface. He will continue his descent until the rotary-wing aircraft actually rests on the water.

FRIES (continued)

With the rear cargo ramp lowered, the Night Stalker pilot of this MH47E sets the helicopter down so the aircraft is literally taking on water. Wave after wave begins to cascade over the ramp and soon the flight engineers are standing in water over the tops of their boots. As the Zodiac begins to line up with the rear of the chopper, the crewmember holds a red-filtered light to signal the team. The Exfil team, guns the engine, ducks their heads, and aims for the ramp and the now flooded fuselage. With a splash and a thud, the team is aboard; already the ramp begins to rise as the helicopter lifts off.

Water flows from the rear of the MH-47E, producing Niagara Falls, 160th style. Once the team has navigated their raft into the helicopter, the pilot will lift off and Exfil the area. As he does so, all the water, which has spilled into the fuselage, will expel from the aircraft.

and secured into the rope at approximately 5-foot intervals. There can be as many as eight rings on the rope. The operators, wearing special harnesses, similar to a parachute harness, will attach themselves to the rope via the rings by clipping in a snap link located at the top of the harness.

Once all team members are secured, a signal is given and the soldiers become airborne in reverse, and extracted out harm's way. This method, is tried and tested. It allows the team members to maintain covering fire from their weapons as they are extracted. Once the team has been whisked out of enemy range and an LZ can be located, the helicopter pilot will bring the troops to ground again. At this time they will disconnect from the rope and board the chopper, which will then complete the extraction.

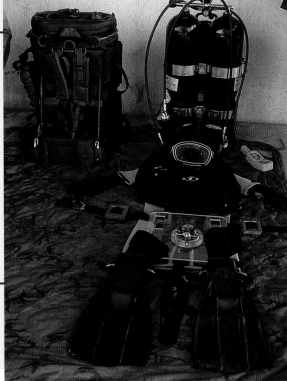

(above) Another method of Infil is via water or rather, under it. Operators will learn the latest techniques in open circuit SCUBA and close circuit, as with the Draeger re-breather. The LAR-V will leave no tell-tale bubbles on the water's surface to give away the operator's location during an underwater insertion.

(right) Open circuit SCUBA equipment is also part of the Delta inventory. Pictured here (from back to front): waterproof rucksack, dual air tanks, gauges, wetsuit, gloves, UDT vest, facemask, compass board, weight belt, fins, and dive knife. Even underwater, an operator is always armed.

(left) Delta operators are skilled in an assortment of Infil methods, whether from sea, air, or land. There is nowhere on the face of the earth the teams cannot get to, and carry out their missions.

Still in use to day is the old UDT vest, which is inflated by a CO_2 cartridge. It also has a backup inflation tube, which is blown up manually.

Aft deck of the Mark V shows the four weapons stations of this special ops watercraft. On the starboard side are mounted two .50-caliber machine guns, while on the port side two Mark 19 40mm machine grenade launchers. A Combat Rubber Raiding Craft (CRRC), or Zodiac, sits poised on the rear deck of the Mark V. The deck is slanted to facilitate the launching and recovery of the CRRC during Infil and extraction operations.

Special Boat Squadrons (SBS) also provide platforms for the insertion of Delta operators. The Mark V is used for insertion and extraction of U.S. SOF. With a speed in excess of 45 knots, and assorted weapons array, the boat crews can lay down suppressive fire in support while extracting operators from a "hot" PZ . Weighing 57 tons per vessel, the Mark V can be delivered in-theater by two C-5 aircraft.

Those members of Delta Force who are Special Forces–qualified are authorized to wear the green beret. Delta members wear the beret flash and crest of the U.S. Army Special Operations Command (Airborne). The USASOC crest bears the inscription *Sine Pari*, defined as "Without Equal."

Support Elements

US Air Force Special Operations Command (AFSOC)

Special Tactics Squadron

Walk down the tarmac at Green Ramp at Pope AFB, or by one of the ranges at Ft. Bragg, and you may see an Air Force sergeant in BDUs, his distinctive patch showing nothing but the Bacardi bat on a black background. He is not the local rum representative stopping by the NCO club to check out its inventory, but rather a member of the elite 24th Special Tactics Squadron. The men of the U.S. Air Force Special Operation Command (AFSOC), Special Tactics Squadrons (STS), have a close working relationship with Delta. In fact the 24th STS is under the Operational Command (OPCON) of JSOC, and that means they're OPCON'd to Delta.

A Special Tactics Team, or STT, is a combination of Combat Controllers (CCT) and Pararescuemen (PJs). These teams are an integral part of the USSOC and its missions. These STTs may function in SR, CSAR, and DA—such as airfield seizure to name just a few of their capabilities. Whatever mission may be assigned to Delta that requires critical air-to-ground coordination, a Special Tactics Team or STT member will be involved. Every member of the STS teams is a volunteer. These highly motivated, proficient STTs are capable of being deployed by sea, air, or land, often weighed down with 100 to 150 pounds of equipment to execute their mission. These units will regularly be found on missions alongside the Delta operators. Whether they HALO in, or infil by fast roping from a Night Stalker MH-60L, STS teams are qualified in the skills that add a lethal element to the Delta teams.

(above) Pararescue Sergeant administers an IV to a wounded team member. Pararescuemen, also known as PJs or ParaJumpers, are highly trained in dealing with the numerous types of injuries as well as the latest methods of trauma medicine. They undergo the same training as U.S. Army Special Forces medics.

(left) A Special Tactics Squadron (STS) Combat Controller (CTT) places an IR signaling light in preparation for a helicopter insertion. STS is a combination of CTTs and Pararescuemen (PJs). These highly trained teams are experts in ATC, CAS, and emergency trauma medicine. Considered an essential element to a successful operation, the 24th STS is OPCON'd to Delta.

Special Tactics Combat Control and Pararescue

Operating under the AFSOC the STS consist of CCT and PJs. These STT are proficient in sea-air-land insertion tactics into forward, non-permissive environments. The CCTs will establish assault zones with an air-traffic-control (ATC) capability. Assault zones could be a DZ for a parachute deployment, or LZ for heliborne operations, or follow-on fixed-wing aircraft. They could also be for an extraction or low-level resupply. Specializing in ATC, when the CCT is given the "go" signal, it can place numerous forms of lights—visible and IR that can be controlled by the CCT members as easily as you would use your TV remote on your home theater system. The CCTs are also responsible for ground-based fire control of the AC-130 Spectre gunships and helicopters of AFSOC, as well as responsibility for *all* air assets, including Army and Navy aircraft. In addition to these capabilities, CCTs provide vital command and control capabilities in the forward AO and are qualified in demolition to remove obstructions and obstacles to the LZ/DZ. It was a

Combat Controller, Major John T. Carney, who performed a recon and surveillance of the Desert One site for the Delta mission in 1980.

The ratio of CCTs to PJs varies with each mission (for example, conducting a CSAR, the team would be PJ "heavy"); however, if the mission were airfield seizure, the team would be made up primarily of CCT. Each mission profile is unique and the STS teams are accomplished in overcoming, adapting, and improvising to meet their objectives. While the CCTs are busy with their tasks, the PJs will be providing any emergency medical care necessary to stabilize and evacuate injured personnel. The PJs of the STS will provide triage and medical treatment for follow-on forces. To say that these individuals are highly skilled would be an understatement. They are instructed in the latest medical procedures in combat and trauma medicine, and attend the Joint Special Operations Medical Training Course, the same as U.S. Army Special Forces Medical Sergeants.

AFSOC Fixed-Wing Aircraft

AC-130U Spectre Gunship

The primary mission of the AC-130U is to deliver precision firepower in support of Close Air Support (CAS) for special operations and conventional ground forces. CAS is defined as air action against hostile targets that are in close proximity to friendly forces and that require detailed integration of each air mission with the fire and movement of those forces. The Spectre can provide accurate fire support with limited collateral damage and can remain on station

An up close and personal view of the 25mm chain cannon. The GAU-12/U 25mm Gatling cannon is full traversable and is also capable of firing 1,800 rpm from extended altitudes of 12,000 feet. The guidance for this weapon is so precise that if you were taking out a truck you could actually request the front or rear tire be targeted.

The AC-130U model Spectre. The U Model has a crew of 13. This particular aircraft is in operation with the 4th Special Operations Squadron at Hurlburt Field, Florida. The Spectre gunships can provide CAS for Delta teams during a DA mission as well as providing covering fire when the team has got to "Get outta Dodge, ASAP!"

Aft weapons array shows the 40mm Bofars and the 105mm Howitzer cannon. Both weapon systems have been upgraded with improved electronics that allow the gunners to fire on two separate targets at the same time. Gunners load ammunition into the Bofors 40mm cannon. The 40mm ammo comes in stacks of 4 per pack and can be continuously fed into the weapon as it fires.

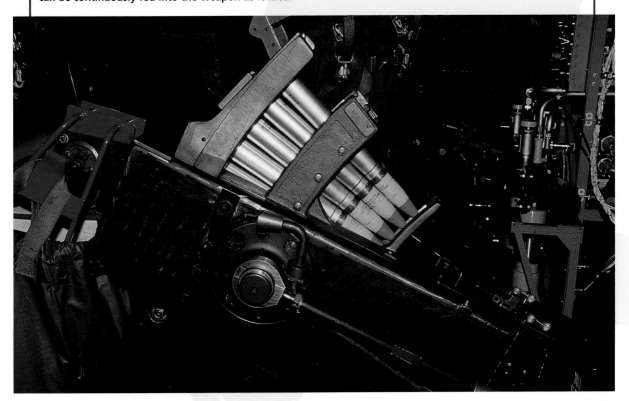

AC-130U Spectre Gunship (continued)

for extended periods of time. These activities are normally carried out under cover of darkness.

The lethality of this gunship is created by three weapon systems. As you enter the AC-130U by way of the front crew hatch and turn to your right, you'll find the GAU-12/U 25mm Gatling cannon that is full traversable and also capable of firing 1,800 rpm from extended altitudes of 12,000 feet. Positioned in the rear of the aircraft are the 40mm Bofors gun and the M102 105mm Howitzer cannon. The 40mm is ideal for providing CAS in "danger close" support to friendly forces due to its small fragmentation pattern. Alongside the Bofors is the M102, 105mm Howitzer cannon, a derivative of the U.S. Army M1A1 howitzer. It has been modified to fire from an aircraft, placed in a special mounting and positioned on the port side of the gunship.

Unlike the "fast movers," that is, F-15s, A-10s, and so on, which must have qualified forward air controllers (FAC) for ordnance delivery in close position to friendly forces, the AC-130U can be controlled by fire-support officers, team leaders, or self-FAC. The fire-control officers are located in the Battle Management Center, or BMC. Here they operate state-of-the-art sensors, navigation, and fire-control systems. These systems, coupled with the trained eyes and skilled hands of their officers, enable the crew to deliver the Spectre's firepower or area saturation with surgical precision—in adverse weather and in total darkness.

(below) A Combat Talon prepares to lift off the tarmac at Hurlburt Field. Encased in that large nose is the AN/APQ-170 Multi Mode Radar (MMR). Directly beneath can be seen the FLIR, allowing the Talon to penetrate hostile airspace. The "E" version is painted in the older camouflage patterns of green. The new color scheme is a matte gray; soon all AFSOC aircraft, both fixed wing and rotary, will be the same color.

The assortment of sensors fitted in this modern gunship consists of an All Light Level Television (ALLTV) system, laser illuminator assembly (LIA), and infrared detection set. A multi-mode radar furnishes exceptionally long-range target direction and identification. This radar is also able to track 40mm and 105mm projectiles and return pinpoint impact locations to the crew for subsequent target adjustment.

MC-130E/H Combat Talon

When their mission calls for a stealthy insertion, Delta operators may load up in one of AFSOC's Combat Talons. The MC-130E Combat Talon I and the MC-130H Combat Talon II are designed for long-range clandestine or covert delivery of special operations forces and equipment. The role of the Combat Talon if to provide global, day, night, and adverse weather capability to airdrop and airland personnel and equipment in support of U.S. and allied special operation forces.

Combat Talons are equipped with forward-looking infrared (FLIR), terrain following/avoidance radars, and specialized aerial-delivery equipment. Incorporated into the Talons are a fully integrated inertial navigation (IIN), global positioning system (GPS), and high-speed aerial delivery system. The Talons use Infrared Flight Rules (IFR), which means the aircraft can be flown in heavy ground fog or low cloud cover when the pilots cannot visually see the ground and must depend on instruments.

These special navigation and aerial delivery systems are employed to locate small drop zones and deliver personnel or equipment with greater accuracy and at higher speeds than possible with a "vanilla" C-130. Such an example would be the insertion of a Delta team operating in a sensitive or hostile territory. MC-130E/H Combat Talons are able to penetrate hostile airspace at low altitudes to carry out these missions. Talon crews are specially trained in night and adverse-weather operations.

MC-130P Combat Shadow

The Combat Shadow extends the range of special-operations helicopters, whether the 160th SOAR(A) or AFSOC assets, by providing air refueling. Operations are conducted primarily in formation, at night, at low level to reduce the probability of visual acquisition and intercept by airborne threats. This is carried out in clandestine or low visibility low-level missions into politically sensitive or hostile territory. The MC-130P may fly in a single or multi-ship mission to reduce detection.

The secondary mission of the Combat Shadow includes the delivery of Delta operators. Small teams, assorted gear, equipment, Zodiacs, and combat rubber raiding craft (CRRC) are a few of the specialized items that are conveyed by the aircraft and its crew. The Shadow is a visual flight rule (VFR) aircraft and would be used when the pilots can see the ground. Penetrations will often utilize radar. Incorporated into the Combat Shadow are IIN and GPS and it has NVG-compatible lighting (interior and exterior). This allows the crew to employ NVG compatible heads-up display (HUD) to fly the plane. It has FLIR, and a missile and radar warning receiver to alert the crew of threats. Countermeasure devices include chaff and flare dispensers. Communications will have satellite and data-burst technology. In addition, the MC-130P will have inflight refueling capability as a receiver.

One of the criticisms of the Holloway commission regarding Operation Eagle Claw was in regard to the method chosen for refueling the helicopters at Desert One. Why wasn't midair refueling used? This capability did exist, as it had been done during the Son Tay raid a decade earlier. The commission believed that, had midair refueling taken place, the disaster would have been avoided. While hindsight is 20/20, it does raise a good point. Consequently, the majority of special operations helicopters today are outfitted with extendable probes, allowing them to be refueled during flight.

An MC-130P Combat Shadow. Note that this Shadow has had the STAR recover arms removed from its nose. The primary function of the MC-130P is to serve as an air re-fueler for AFSOC and Night Stalker helicopters. It can also be used as an insertion platform for delivery of Delta teams into denied or hostile territories.

AFSOC Helicopters

MH-53M Pave Low III E

The mission of the MH-53M is carry out low-level, long-range, undetected ingress into denied or hostile areas. This is accomplished day or night, even under the worst weather conditions for infiltration, exfiltration, and re-supply of special operations forces. Equipped with FLIR, inertial GPS, Doppler navigation systems, terrain following/avoidance radars, on-board computer, and integrated advanced avionics, it is able to achieve precise, low-level, long-range penetration into denied areas without detection day or night, in adverse weather; and over hazardous terrain.

MH-53M Pave Low is equipped with Interactive Defensive Avionics System/Multi-Mission Advanced Tactical Terminal (IDAS/MATT). This modification will provide the aircrews with a heightened level of readiness and efficiency. This system is a color, multi-functional, night-vision-compatible digital map screen. Located on the helicopter's instrument panel, the display gives the crew a more concise view of the battlefield. Crew members will

(top right) Newly upgraded MH-53M Pave Low. Modified with the Interactive Defense Avionics System/Multi-Mission Advance Tactical Terminal (IDAS/MATT).

(below) Starboard gunner of the Pave Low engages the minigun. This 7.62mm minigun is capable of putting 2,000 or 4,000 rpm on target. This is a welcome asset during a hot extraction and the gunner lays down a protective stream of lead while the team rapidly boards the helicopter.

MH-53M Pave Low III E (continued)

have instant access to real-time events. This includes the helicopter's flight path, manmade obstacles, such as power lines, and even hostile threats "over the horizon."

Armor plating and an assortment of weapons systems offer protection to the crew. Just aft of the flight deck are two 7.62mm miniguns, and at the rear of the helicopter on the exit ramp a .50 caliber machine gun is located. While the mission of the Pave Low is primarily an Infil/Exfil platform, with all the previously mentioned weapons, it also serves as a helicopter gunship.

Located on the rear cargo ramp of the Pave Low, a gunner operates the M-2 .50-caliber machine gun. The M2 is a formidable weapon against troops, bunkers, and soft skinned vehicles, such as Armored Personnel Carriers (APCs). The gunner braces himself as the 92-foot helicopter banks to the right.

CV-22 Osprey

The CV-22 Osprey, born out of the issues raised by the Holloway Commission. Conceptually, it takes off and hovers like a helicopter then transitions to fly like an airplane. Some call the Osprey the savior of special ops air platforms, referring to it as a rock solid aircraft; others just refer to it as a rock. It seems there is a problem with the CV-22 staying in the air. All new aircraft have their "bugs"; time will tell whether the CV-22 is an asset or an albatross. *Bell/Boeing*

The controversial Osprey: part plane, part helicopter. Currently planned as a replacement for the aging fleet of MH-53 Pave Lows and some of the MC-130 aircraft. It has the capability of providing a long-range Infil/Exfil platform for Delta Force as they head into the turbulent War on Terrorism. *Bell/Boeing*

The Osprey is a tilt-rotor vertical lift aircraft, which means it takes off like a helicopter and flies like a conventional airplane. There is nothing conventional about the Osprey, however. Development of the V-22 program—designated the MV-22—began in 1981; it was originally designed for the U.S. Marines. Planned for introduction into AFSOC forces in 2003, the CV-22 will be a special operations variant of the MV-22. The mission of the CV-22 will be Infil/Exfil and resupply special operations forces in denied or enemy areas, in total darkness in all weather.

The CV-22 differs from the MV-22 with the addition of a third seat in the cockpit for a flight engineer. It will also be fitted with a refueling probe to facilitate midair refueling. Additionally, the AFSOC version of the Osprey will have the modern suite of electronics, (including items such as a multi-mode terrain avoidance and terrain-following radar) like those installed in other AFSOC aircraft. To deal with the nature of special operations, it will have enhanced electronic warning (EW) equipment for increased battlefield awareness. It will be equipped with more than 2.5 times the volume of flares and chaff, radar jamming gear, and improved integration of defensive countermeasures. For CSAR it will have an internally mounted rescue hoist and a crew door located on the starboard side of the aircraft. Another significant difference between the AFSOC and the Marine version will be the amount of fuel it will carry; the CV-22 will have approximately twice the fuel capacity of the MV-22 variant.

160th Special Operations Aviation Regiment (Airborne)

Renowned for having some of the best helicopter pilots in the world, SOAR(A) provides aviation support to U.S. Special Operations Forces. Since many of their missions are carried out under cover of darkness, the unit has earned the sobriquet "The Night Stalkers." It was the unit of choice for such operations as Operation Acid Gambit, Panama, and in Mogadishu, Somalia. Primarily an Army asset, the 160th has a close working relationship with other units under the SOCOM command. Capabilities of the 160th SOAR(A) include the use of dedicated aviation assets to accomplish clandestine penetration for insertion, extraction, and resupply. The regiment may also conduct armed escort, reconnaissance, surveillance, and electronic warfare in support of missions.

The Night Stalkers maintain several types of helicopters in their inventory, from the small and agile "Little Birds" to the large size "Chinooks." Whether Delta needs to perform a FRIES on a rooftop, request CAS, or extract from a "hot" LZ, the 160th SOAR(A) has the aircraft, pilots, and aircrews to accomplish the task. The unit's motto is "Night Stalkers Don't Quit!" The consummate flyers are the perfect complement to the covert warriors of Delta.

MH-6J "Little Bird"

The MH-6J is a single-engine light utility helicopter similar to the Vietnam era OH-6 "Loach." Based on the Hughes 500 Defender series, and the MH-6J currently manufactured by MD Helicopters, it has been modified with outboard platforms on both sides of the aircraft, a configuration referred to as the External Personnel System, which can accommodate a total of six external and two internal seating positions. The helicopter is capable of conducting covert Infil/Exfil, and combat assaults over varying terrain and weather conditions. In addition to its Infil/Exfil roles, it is also used for reconnaissance missions and command and control. Its compact size allows for rapid deployment in C-130, C-141, C-17, and C-5 transport aircraft. Some aircraft are equipped with FLIR, a passive system that provides an infrared image of terrain features as well as ground or airborne objects. The aircraft can be configured for Fast Roping operations, as well as adding special racks to provide the capability to insert and extract up to two motorcycles.

All crews are qualified to conduct NVG infil and exfil, STABO, Fast Rope, and aerial suppression operations to urban, mountainous, desert, and jungle objectives, as well as to ships and offshore drilling platforms. Crews are trained in long-range precision navigation and formation flight over land and water to arrive at objectives at a prearranged time (+ 30 seconds). Maximum range (with two auxiliary tanks installed) is 400 nautical miles. Mission endurance (with 1 auxiliary tank installed) is three hours, 20 minutes (including a 20-minute reserve). Maximum endurance (with two auxiliary tanks installed) is five hours (including the 20-minute reserve).

> **Any Air Force transport aircraft can deploy the MH-6. A C-141 is capable of transporting up to 6 MH-6s and a C-130 is able to transport up to 3 MH-6s, with a rapid upload/offload capability. The MH-6s can offload, build up, and depart within 15 minutes. Self-deployment is unlimited, provided there is refuel support at ground or surface vessel locations every 270 nautical miles. It is useful in the insertion of teams during CT or DA missions. *Richard Marshall***

AH-6J Light Attack Helicopter

The AH-6J LAH is a highly modified version of the McDonnell Douglas 530 series commercial helicopter. The aircraft is a single-turbine-engine, dual-flight-control, light attack helicopter. It is primarily employed in close air support of ground troops, target destruction raids, and armed escort of other aircraft. A controllable infrared surveillance system provides the pilots a TV video-type of infrared image of terrain features and ground. The FLIR detects long wavelength radiant IR energy emitted, naturally or artificially, by any object in daylight or darkness. The helicopter has a wide range of weaponry, ranging from 7.62mm miniguns, to "Hellfire" Anti-tank Guided Missiles.

(right) The AH-6J is capable of mounting a variety of weapons systems. Normal aircraft configuration consists of two 7.62mm miniguns with 1,500 to 2,000 rounds per gun, and two 7-shot 2.75-inch rocket pods. The following are additional configurations: The M134 7.62mm Minigun is a 6-barrel, air-cooled, link-fed, electrically-driven Gatling gun. The weapon has a rate of fire of 2,000 or 4,000 rpm, with a range of 100 to 750 meters. *Richard Marshall*

(below) M261 seven tube Rocket Launcher. This system fires a 2.75-inch Folding Fin Aerial Rocket (FFAR) with a variety of special purpose warheads. The 2.75-inch FFAR can be used as a point target weapon at ranges from 100 to 750 meters and an area fire weapon at ranges up to 7,000 meters. *Richard Marshall*

Heralded as the "best pilots in the world" they redefined the discipline of long-range, low-level penetration. The skill and experience of the Night Stalker pilots coupled with the advanced integrated avionics suite with: a MIL Standard 1553B data bus architecture, FLIR and radar sensors, and an air-refueling capability bring Infil/Exfil to a new level of excellence.

MH-60 Blackhawk

The 160th SOAR(A) operates three Blackhawk variants: The MH-60K (Blackhawk) is a version of the Sikorsky UH-60 utility helicopter that has been modified especially for special-operations missions. These modifications include an aerial refueling (AR) capability, a sophisticated collection of aircraft survivability equipment (ASE), and improved navigation systems that allow the helicopter to operate in the most austere environments and adverse weather conditions.

The MH-60K is a hybrid derivative of the field-proven UH-60A Blackhawk. The helicopter is powered by twin General Electric T700-GE-701C turboshaft engines rated at 1,700 shp each, plus the 3,400 shp, an improved durability gearbox, and aerial refueling capability in a variety of tank configurations. It has a digital automatic flight control computer with coupled automatic approach/depart/hover functions and specifically designed airframe and landing gear features for a high degree of battlefield survivability. It also has hardened flight controls; redundant electrical and hydraulic systems; a self-sealing, crash-resistant fuel system; and energy-absorbing landing gear and crew seats. With fully integrated cockpit and avionics, it is capable of precise navigation, day or night, in all types weather conditions.

The second variant is the MH-60L, whose primary mission is to carry out Infil, Exfil, and resupply operations in a variety of environmental conditions. Secondary missions of the MH-60 include external load, CSAR, and MEDEVAC operations. The MH-60 can operate from a fixed base, remote sites, or on a ship.

Finally, the MH-60L Direct Action Penetrator (DAP) is equipped with an assortment of weapons systems. The DAP has the primary mission of armed escort and fire support. Its mission is to conduct CAS, employing precision-guided ordnance in the support of Infil or Exfil of small units. The DAP can be called upon to perform any mission day or night, in all types of adverse weather conditions.

(right) Pitch-black night. Adverse weather. Hostile territory. Just another "day at the office" for the pilots of the 160th SOAR(A) as they put this MH-60K through its paces. This L model Blackhawk is fitted with an extendable probe to facilitate mid-air refueling. *Richard Marshall*

(below) MH-60L DAP (Direct Action Penetrator) is capable of mounting two M-134 7.62mm miniguns, two 30mm Chain-Guns, two 19-shot 2.75 rocket pods, and Hellfire and Stinger missiles in a variety of combinations, depending on mission parameters. An integrated fire control system, combined with the pilot's head-up display (HUD) makes the DAP a precision weapons delivery platform operational both day and night. The standard configuration of the DAP is one rocket pod, one 30mm cannon, and two miniguns. *Richard Marshall*

MH-60 Blackhawk (continued)

The M134 7.62mm Minigun is a 6 barrel, air-cooled, link fed, electrically-driven Gatling gun, with a 1000-meter maximum effective range. The M261 19 tube Rocket Launcher fires a 2.75-inch folding fin aerial rocket with a variety of special purpose warheads, including: 10-pound and 17-pound high explosive (HE) warheads for light armor and bunker penetration, anti-personnel flechette warhead, white phosphorous, white and IR illumination warheads. M230 30mm Chain Gun is a rapid-fire cannon capable of firing 625 rounds of High Explosive Dual Purpose (HEDP) per minute at ranges out to 4,000 meters. The DAP may also carry the Hellfire semi-active laser guided missile, capable of defeating any known armor. The M272 launchers are able to hold four Hellfire missiles each. The missile can be designated by any ground or air NATO standard laser designator. *Richard Marshall*

MH-47 Chinook

The primary mission of the MH-47 is overt and covert Infil, Exfil, air assault, and resupply of SOF teams, including Delta. The MH-47 helicopter delivered Delta teams and their FAVs to remote LZs in Iraq to hunt down the elusive Scuds. The 160th SOAR(A) currently operates two models: the MH-47D Adverse Weather Cockpit (AWC), which is capable of operating at night during the worst of weather conditions. With the use of special mission equipment and night vision devices, the aircrew can operate in hostile mission environments over all types of terrain at low altitudes during periods of low visibility and low ambient lighting conditions with pinpoint navigation accuracy; achieved by the employment of the aircrafts; Forward Looking Infrared (FLIR); and a navigation system consisting of a Mission Computer employing GPS/INS/Doppler navigation. The weapons array includes two M-134 machine guns and one M-60D machine gun located on the rear loading ramp.

The newest Chinook is the MH-47E, nicknamed the "Dark Horse." This heavy assault helicopter, like its sister ship, was specifically designed to support SOF missions. It has totally integrated avionics subsystems and the combination of backup avionics architecture with dual mission processors, remote terminal units, multifunction displays, and display generators to improve combat survivability and mission reliability; it has an A/R probe for midair refueling, an external rescue hoist, and two L714 turbine engines. The aircraft's fuel tanks are integral, replacing the internal auxiliary fuel tanks usually carried on the MH-47D and providing 2,068 gallons of fuel with no loss of cargo space. Crewmembers for both MH-47 variants include a pilot, co-pilot, flight engineer, and two crew chiefs.

(left) The MH-47E's Integrated Avionics System (IAS) permits global communications and navigation. The IAS is the most advanced system of its kind ever installed in a U.S. Army helicopter. The IAS includes FLIR and MMR for nap-of-the-earth and low-level flight operations in conditions of extremely poor visibility and adverse weather. *Richard Marshall*

(below) When the mission calls for covert insertion and extraction of a team and an FAV, at low level, day or night, in adverse weather, over any type of terrain, the Night Stalkers will fire up one of their MH-47E helicopters. The USASOC equipped the 160th SOAR(A) with MH-47Es based at Fort Campbell, Kentucky, and Hunter Army Airfield, Savannah, Georgia.

Author's Notes

Into the Future, into the Shadows

As we enter the new millennium, the Cold War has been over for more than a decade. The old threat of a conventional war in Europe fades into memory, without even one Soviet T-80 battle tank marring the soil of the Fulda Gap. Today, however, the continued threat of international terrorism born out of the turbulent 1970s still asserts its demonic presence. The horrendous attack on the World Trade Center in New York City and the Pentagon in Washington, D.C., on 11 September 2001, by a band of godless cowards has brought terrorism to American soil anew. Gone is the large Russian bear, replaced by a plethora of diminutive, dissolute dictators, murderous thugs and heathens trying to establish their place in history; and individuals who seek to oppress their people, conquer their neighbors and subjugate the world to their foolish notions.

While the geopolitical clime adapts from conflict to conflict, the teams of Delta Force have also been refining their skills over the past quarter-century. This ultra-elite force of dedicated warriors constitutes America's Samurai: honed to a razor's edge as much as the knives they carry are. The Delta teams stand ready, whether called upon to extract a hostage from harm's way or mete out National Command Authority orders with precision assaults upon enemies of the United States. They shall do so with fervor never imagined by our enemies, bringing "unholiness" to any so-called Jihad. My only advice to those purveyors of evil would be this: "These teams are going to hit the ground with a sense of purpose and a really 'bad attitude' regarding any enemy of freedom. This is one unit you do not want to bump into in the middle of the night," and I believe those in Delta would say, "Roger that!"

In the previous chapters we have shown some of the tools of the trade used to strike blows for liberty and freedom. This has been a sampling of the weapons, not an exhaustive study. Delta Force is assiduously on the cutting edge when it comes to technology in C4I, and state-of-the-art in the lethality of their weapons. Nevertheless, it is the operator who makes the difference. Whether armed with a SOPMOD M4A1 carbine, or Randall knife, they will "drive on," for theirs is the soul of a warrior.

To those who shall remain in the shadows, we, the protected and free, say "Thank you."

Glossary

AT: Antiterrorism. Defensive measures used to reduce the vulnerability of individuals and property to terrorism.

Clandestine Operation: Activities sponsored or conducted by governmental departments or agencies in such a way as to assure secrecy or concealment. (It differs from covert operations in that emphasis is placed on concealment of the operation rather than on concealment of identity of sponsor.) In Special Operations, an activity may be both covert and clandestine and may focus equally on operational considerations and intelligence-related activities.

Close Air Support (CAS): Air action against hostile targets that are in close proximity to friendly forces and that require detailed integration of each air mission with the fire and movement of those forces.

Counterproliferation: Activities taken to counter the spread of dangerous military capabilities, allied technologies and/or know-how, especially weapons of mass destruction and ballistic missile delivery systems.

CT: Counterterrorism. Offensive measures taken to prevent, deter, and respond to terrorism.

Covert Operations: Operations that are so planned and executed as to conceal the identity of, or permit plausible denial by, the sponsor.

Crisis: An incident or situation involving a threat to the United States, its territories, citizens, military forces and possessions, or vital interests that develops rapidly and creates a condition of such diplomatic, economic, political, or military importance that commitment of U.S. military forces and resources is contemplated to achieve national objectives.

Direct action mission: In special operations, a specified act involving operations of an overt, covert, clandestine or low-visibility nature conducted primarily by a sponsoring power's special operations forces in hostile or denied areas.

Exfiltration (Exfil): The removal of personnel or units from areas under enemy control.

Humanitarian assistance: Assistance provided by Department of Defense forces, as directed by appropriate authority, in the aftermath of natural or manmade disasters to help reduce conditions that present a serious threat to life and property. Assistance provided by U.S. forces is limited in scope and duration and is designed to supplement efforts of civilian authorities that have primary responsibility for providing such assistance.

Infiltration (Infil): The movement through or into an area or territory occupied by either friendly or enemy troops or organizations. The movement is made either by small groups or by individuals at extended or irregular intervals. When used in connection with the enemy, it implies that contact is avoided.

Insurgency: An organized movement aimed at the overthrow of a constituted government through the use of subversion and armed conflict.

Internal defense: The full range of measures taken by a government to free and protect its society from subversion, lawlessness, and insurgency.

Inter-operability: The ability of systems, units, or forces to provide services to, and to and accept services from, other systems, units, or forces and/or use the services so exchanged to enable them to operate effectively together.

Low-intensity conflict: Political-military confrontation between contending states or groups below conventional war and above routine, peaceful competition among states. It frequently involves protracted struggles between competing principles and ideologies. Low-intensity conflict ranges from subversion to the use of armed force. It is waged by a combination of means employing political, economic, informational, and military instruments. Low-intensity conflicts are often localized, generally in the Third World, but contain regional and global security implications.

Mission: A statement of our reason for being and what we wish to accomplish as an organization.

NCA: National Command Authorities. The President and the Secretary of Defense together, or their duly deputized alternates or successors. The term signifies constitutional authority to direct the Armed Forces in their execution of military action.

Objectives: Specific actions to be achieved in a specified time period. Accomplishment will indicate progress toward achieving the goals.

Operator: Delta Force Shooter

Psychological operations: Planned operations to convey selected information and indicators to foreign audiences to influence their emotions, motives, objective reasoning, and ultimately the behavior of foreign governments, organizations, groups, and individuals. The purpose of psychological operations is to induce or reinforce foreign attitudes and behavior favorable to the originator's objectives.

Shooter: Special Operations Forces trooper, i.e., Delta Operator, U.S. Army Special Forces, U.S. Navy SEAL, U.S. Army Ranger, SAS, etc.

Special Reconnaissance: Reconnaissance and surveillance actions conducted by special operations forces to obtain or verify, by visual observation or other collection methods, information concerning the capabilities, intentions, and activities of an actual or potential enemy or to secure data concerning the meteorological, hydrographic, or geographic characteristics of a particular area. It includes target acquisition, area assessment and post-strike reconnaissance.

Strategy: Methods, approaches, or specific moves taken to implement and attain an objective.

Abbreviations and Acronyms

AAA	Anti-Aircraft Artillery	**FAC**	Forward Air Controller
AAR	After Action Report	**FAV**	Fast Attack Vehicle
ACOG	Advance Combat Optical Gunsight	**FFAR**	Folding-Fin Aerial Rocket
AFSOC	Air Force Special Operations Command	**FLIR**	Forward-Looking Infrared
AGL	Above Ground Level	**FRIES**	Fast Rope Insertion/Extraction System
ALLTV	All Light Level Television	**GPS**	Global Positioning System
AO	Area of Operations	**HAHO**	High-Altitude, High-Opening
APC	Armored Personnel Carrier	**HALO**	High-Altitude, Low-Opening
AR	Aerial Refueling	**HDS**	Holographic Display Sight
ARD	Anti-Reflective Device	**HE**	High Explosive
ARSOC	Army Special Operations Command	**HEDP**	High Explosive Dual Purpose
ASE	Aircraft Survivability Equipment	**HK**	Heckler and Koch
AT-4	Anti-Tank Weapon	**HTI**	Hard Target Interdiction
ATC	Air-Traffic-Control	**HUD**	Heads-Up-Display
AWC	Adverse Weather Cockpit	**HUMMV**	Humvee
BAC	Bindon Aiming Concept	**IAS**	Integrated Avionics System
BIS	Backup Iron Sight	**IC**	Integrated Carbine
BMC	Battle Management Center	**IDAS/MATT**	Interactive Defensive Avionics System/Multi-Mission Advanced Tactical Terminal
BMG	Browning Machine Gun		
C&C	Command and Control		
C4I	Command, Control, Communication, Computers and Intelligence	**IFR**	Infrared Flight Rules
		IIN	Integrated Inertial Navigation
CAG	Combat Applications Group	**IR**	Infrared
CAS	Close Air Support	**ISA**	Intelligence Support Activity
CCT	Combat Controllers	**ITPIAL**	Infrared Target Pointer/Illuminator/Aiming Laser
CENTCOM	Central Command		
CIA	Central Intelligence Agency	**JCS**	Joint Chiefs of Staff
CID	Combat Identification	**JSOC**	Joint Special Operations Command
CinC	Commander in Chief	**JSOTF**	Joint Special Operations Task Force
COMSEC	Communications Security	**LAM**	Laser Aiming Module
COTS	Commercial Off The Shelf	**LAW**	Light Anti-Tank Weapon
CQB	Close-Quarters Battle	**LBE**	Load-Bearing Equipment
CRE	Close-Range Engagement	**LIA**	Laser Illuminator Assembly
CRRC	Combat Rubber Raiding Craft	**LOS**	Line Of Sight
CSAR	Combat Search and Rescue	**LSS**	Lightweight Shotgun System
CT	Counterterrorism	**LZ**	Landing Zone
CTJTF	Counter Terrorism Joint Task Force	**MBITR**	Multiband Inter/Intra Team Radio
DA	Direct Action	**MFF**	Military Free Fall
DAM/T	Direct Action Mission/Team	**MMR**	Multi-Mode Radio
DAMA	Demand Assigned Multiple Access	**MNVS**	Mini Night Vision Sight
DAP	Direct Action Penetrator	**MOA**	Minute Of Angle
DOAV	Delta Operator's Assault Vest	**MOH**	Medal Of Honor
DOD	Department of Defense	**MOS**	Military Occupational Specialty
DPV	Desert Patrol Vehicle	**MOUT**	Military Operations Urban Terrain
DZ	Drop Zone	**MSHR**	Miniature Secure Handheld Radio
E&E	Evasion and Escape	**MSL**	Mean Sea Level
ECOS	Enhanced Combat Optical Sight	**MUGR**	Miniature Underwater GPS Receiver
EFP	Explosively Formed Penetrator	**NSA**	National Security Agency

NVD	Night Vision Device
NVG	Night-Vision Goggles
OPCON/M	Operational Control/Command
OPSEC	Operational Security
OSS	Office of Strategic Service
OTC	Operators Training Course
PAM	Penetration Augmented Munition
PBX	Plastic-Bonded Explosive
PDW	Personal Defense Weapon
PJ	Pararescuemen
PPS	Precise Positioning Service
PTT	Push-To-Talk
QAD	Quick Attach/Detach
QRF	Quick Reaction Force
RAPS	Ram Air Parachute System
RAS	Rail adapter System
RATT	Rapid All Terrain Transport
RFD	Radio Firing Device
RIS	Rail Interface System
RPG	Rocket-Propelled Grenade
RPM	Rounds Per Minute
S&W	Smith & Wesson
SAS	Special Air Service (U.K. or Australian)
SATCOM	Satellite Communications
SAW	Squad Automatic Weapon
SBS	Special Boat Squadron (U.K.)
SDGPS	Secure Differential GPS
SEAL	Sea Air Land (U.S. Navy Special Operations Forces)
SERE	Survival, Escape, Resistance, and Evasion
SF	Special Forces (U.S. Army)
SLAM	Selectable Lightweight Attack Munition
SOAP	Special Operations Advisory Panel
SOAR(A)	160th Special Operations Aviation Regiment (Airborne)
SOCOM	Special Operations Command
SOF	Special Operations Forces
SOFLAM	Special Operations Forces Laser Acquisition Marker
SOP	Standard Operating Practice
SOPMOD	Special Operations Peculiar Modification
SOTIC	Special Operations Target Interdiction Course
SPS	Standard Positioning Service
SR	Special Reconnaissance
STS	Special Tactics Squadron
STT	Special Tactics Team
SWS	Sniper Weapon System

TDFD	Time Delay Firing Device
TEL	Transport, Erector, Launcher
TF	Task Force
TFR	Task Force Ranger
TGO	Terminal-Guided Ordnance
TNAZ	Trinitroazetidine
UNOSOM	United Nations Operations in Somalia
USASOC	U.S. Army Special Operations Command
USSOCOM	U.S. Special Operation Command
VFR	Visual Flight Rule
VL	Visible Laser
VLI	Visible Light Illuminator
WAGE	Wide Area GPS Enhancement

Index

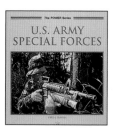
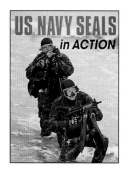
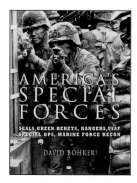
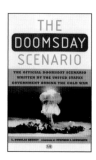

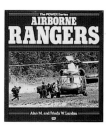